The Life Cycle of Butterflies

TEACHER'S GUIDE

SCIENCE AND TECHNOLOGY FOR CHILDREN™

NATIONAL SCIENCE RESOURCES CENTER
Smithsonian Institution • National Academy of Sciences
Arts and Industries Building, Room 1201
Washington, DC 20560

The National Science Resources Center is operated by the Smithsonian Institution and the National Academy of Sciences to improve the teaching of science in the nation's schools. The NSRC collects and disseminates information about exemplary teaching resources, develops and disseminates curriculum materials, and sponsors outreach activities, specifically in the areas of leadership development and technical assistance, to help school districts develop and sustain hands-on science programs.

STC Project Supporters

National Science Foundation
Smithsonian Institution
U.S. Department of Defense
U.S. Department of Education
John D. and Catherine T. MacArthur Foundation
The Dow Chemical Company Foundation
E. I. du Pont de Nemours & Company
Amoco Foundation, Inc.
Hewlett-Packard Company
Smithsonian Institution Educational Outreach Fund
Smithsonian Women's Committee

This project was supported, in part,
by the
National Science Foundation
Opinions expressed are those of the authors
and not necessarily those of the Foundation

ISBN 0-89278-617-5

Published by Carolina Biological Supply Company, 2700 York Road, Burlington, NC 27215.
Call toll free 800-334-5551.

This material is based upon work supported by the National Science Foundation under Grant No. ESI-9252947. Any opinions, findings, and conclusions or recommendations expressed in this material are those of the author(s) and do not necessarily reflect the views of the National Science Foundation.

CB787100004

♻ Printed on recycled paper.

Foreword

Since 1988, the National Science Resources Center (NSRC) has been developing Science and Technology for Children (STC), an innovative hands-on science program for children in grades one through six. The 24 units of the STC program, four for each grade level, are designed to provide all students with stimulating experiences in the life, earth, and physical sciences and technology while simultaneously developing their critical-thinking and problem-solving skills.

Sequence of STC Units

Grade	Life, Earth, and Physical Sciences and Technology			
1	Organisms	Weather	Solids and Liquids	Comparing and Measuring
2	The Life Cycle of Butterflies	Soils	Changes	Balancing and Weighing
3	Plant Growth and Development	Rocks and Minerals	Chemical Tests	Sound
4	Animal Studies	Land and Water	Electric Circuits	Motion and Design
5	Microworlds	Ecosystems	Food Chemistry	Floating and Sinking
6	Experiments with Plants	Measuring Time	Magnets and Motors	The Technology of Paper

The STC units provide children with the opportunity to learn age-appropriate concepts and skills and to acquire scientific attitudes and habits of mind. In the primary grades, children begin their study of science by observing, measuring, and identifying properties. Then they move on through a progression of experiences that culminate in grade six with the design of controlled experiments.

Sequence of Development of Scientific Reasoning Skills

Scientific Reasoning Skills	Grades					
	1	2	3	4	5	6
Observing, Measuring, and Identifying Properties	◆	◆	◆	◆	◆	◆
Seeking Evidence Recognizing Patterns and Cycles		◆	◆	◆	◆	◆
Identifying Cause and Effect Extending the Senses				◆	◆	◆
Designing and Conducting Controlled Experiments						◆

The "Focus-Explore-Reflect-Apply" learning cycle incorporated into the STC units is based on research findings about children's learning. These findings indicate that knowledge is actively constructed by each learner and that children learn science best in a hands-on experimental environment where they can make their own discoveries. The steps of the learning cycle are as follows:

■ Focus: Explore and clarify the ideas that children already have about the topic.

■ Explore: Enable children to engage in hands-on explorations of the objects, organisms, and science phenomena to be investigated.

■ Reflect: Encourage children to discuss their observations and to reconcile their ideas.

■ Apply: Help children discuss and apply their new ideas in new situations.

The learning cycle in STC units gives students opportunities to develop increased understanding of important scientific concepts and to develop positive attitudes toward science.

The STC units provide teachers with a variety of strategies with which to assess student learning. The STC units also offer teachers opportunities to link the teaching of science with the development of skills in mathematics, language arts, and social studies. In addition, the STC units encourage the use of cooperative learning to help students develop the valuable skill of working together.

In the extensive research and development process used with all STC units, scientists and educators, including experienced elementary school teachers, act as consultants to teacher-developers, who research, trial teach, and write the units. The process begins with the developer researching the unit's content and pedagogy. Then, before writing the unit, the developer trial teaches lessons in public school classrooms in the metropolitan Washington, D.C., area. Once a unit is written, the NSRC evaluates its effectiveness with children by field-testing it nationally in ethnically diverse urban, rural, and suburban public schools. At the field-testing stage, the assessment sections in each unit are also evaluated by the Program Evaluation and Research Group of Lesley College, located in Cambridge, Mass. The final editions of the units reflect the incorporation of teacher and student field-test feedback and of comments on accuracy and soundness from the leading scientists and science educators who serve on the STC Advisory Panel.

The STC project would not have been possible without the generous support of numerous federal agencies, private foundations, and corporations. Supporters include the National Science Foundation, the Smithsonian Institution, the U.S. Department of Defense, the U.S. Department of Education, the John D. and Catherine T. MacArthur Foundation, the Dow Chemical Company Foundation, the Amoco Foundation, Inc., E. I. du Pont de Nemours & Company, the Hewlett-Packard Company, the Smithsonian Institution Educational Outreach Fund, and the Smithsonian Women's Committee.

Acknowledgments

The primary authors of *The Life Cycle of Butterflies* were Seliesa Pembleton and Patricia McGlashan. They are deeply indebted to Richard McQueen, specialist, science education, Multnomah Education Service District, Portland, Oregon. He was an important source of information and support, giving generously of his time and talent. Mr. McQueen developed a butterflies unit and has used it for years in his school district. That unit served as the inspiration for this one. *The Life Cycle of Butterflies* was edited by Marilyn Fenichel and illustrated by Max-Karl Winkler. Other NSRC staff who contributed to the development and production of this unit include Sally Goetz Shuler, deputy director; Joe Griffith, STC project director; Kathleen Johnston, publications director; and Timothy Falb, publications technology specialist. The unit was evaluated by George Hein and Sabra Price, Program Evaluation and Research Group, Lesley College.

In developing the unit, Ms. Pembleton and Ms. McGlashan worked with a number of individuals from the Smithsonian Institution:

Richard Efthim, Manager, Naturalist Center
The Entomology and Botany Libraries staffs of the Natural History Libraries
Sally Love, Director, Insect Zoo
The staff of the Office of Horticulture
Barbara van Creveld, Program Manager, Insect Zoo

Many people contributed to the national field-testing of *The Life Cycle of Butterflies*. The following individuals coordinated the testing:

Gerry Consuegra, Science Coordinator, Mongomery County Public Schools, Division of Academic Skills, Rockville, MD
Rosemarie Holland, Science Coordinator, Boyd Elementary School, Alamosa School District, Alamosa, CO

Gladys Morgan, Principal, Petworth Elementary School, District of Columbia Public Schools, Washington, DC
Judy Reid, Science Resource Teacher, Anchorage School District, Anchorage, AK

The NSRC would also like to thank the following individuals and school systems for their assistance with the national field-testing of the unit:

In the Montgomery County School District:
Ann Burk, Stonegate Elementary School; Diane Creel, Cedar Grove Elementary School; Dawn Eddy, McKenney Hills Elementary School; Lynn Ferrell, Strawberry Knoll Elementary School; Jennifer Gilbert, Maryvale Elementary School; Barbara Gold, McKenney Hills Elementary School; Saundra Groner, Stonegate Elementary School; Linda Hepner, Cedar Grove Elementary School; Pat Howell, Burtonsville Elementary School; Marilyn Knowles, Somerset Elementary School; Susan Little, Burtonsville Elementary School; Katie Livingston, Cedar Grove Elementary School; Margaret Manley, Stonegate Elementary School; Marjorie P. Walsh, Potomac Elementary School; Gail Potter, Stonegate Elementary School; Roberta Robbins, Rosemont Elementary School; Barbara Rubin, Rosemont Elementary School; Debra Trester, Ritchie Park Elementary School

In the Alamosa School District:
Colleen Bennett, Louise Claflin, Peggy Herrera, Teena McGuire, Mary Motz, Agnes Rivera, Sue Robinson, and Bertha Trujillo, Boyd Elementary School

In the District of Columbia Public Schools:
Streata Yarborough, Petworth Elementary School

In the Anchorage School District:
David Gillam, Susitna Elementary School; Jody Martinez, Muldoon Elementary School; Cathy Morgan, O'Malley Elementary School

Douglas Lapp
Executive Director
National Science Resources Center

STC Advisory Panel

Contents

Goals for *The Life Cycle of Butterflies*

In this unit, students observe the life cycle of the Painted Lady butterfly. Through their experiences, they are introduced to the following concepts, skills, and attitudes.

Concepts

- The different stages of a butterfly's life cycle are egg, larva, caterpillar, chrysalis, and adult.

- Caterpillars need food, air, and space to live and grow.

- The caterpillar forms a chrysalis, and a butterfly emerges from the chrysalis.

- A butterfly needs food to live, but it does not grow after emerging from the chrysalis.

- A butterfly lays eggs, which hatch into larvae.

Skills

- Observing, describing, and recording growth and change in the larva.

- Predicting, comparing, and discussing the larva's appearance and change over time.

- Communicating observations through drawing and writing.

- Relating observations of the butterfly's life cycle to students' own growth and change.

- Extending knowledge of butterflies through reading.

Attitudes

- Developing an interest in studying insects.

- Appreciating the needs of living things.

- Valuing scientific information that has been collected over time.

Unit Overview and Materials List

The *Life Cycle of Butterflies* is a four- to six-week unit designed and tested for 2nd graders that highlights the life cycle of the Painted Lady butterfly (*Vanessa cardui*). This butterfly is especially well suited for classroom study. It is small and brightly colored, will accept a variety of foods, is found worldwide, and undergoes complete metamorphosis in a relatively short time (from three to four weeks, depending on the temperature).

The main objective of the unit is to introduce young children to the concept of life cycles by using one organism as an example. Students also learn observational and recording skills, and add to their scientific vocabulary.

The first eight lessons focus on caterpillar and chrysalis stages of the Painted Lady butterfly. Students begin their study of these two stages by sharing their prior knowledge of caterpillars and then, as a pre-assessment exercise, they draw what they think a caterpillar looks like. In Lesson 2, they learn about caterpillars' basic needs for air, water, food, and shelter and make and record their first observations.

In Lessons 3 through 6, emphasis is placed on developing observational and recording skills. Students watch the caterpillars as they crawl, hang upside down, spin silk, eat and eliminate waste (frass), rest, and shed skin (molt).

In Lessons 7 and 8, the caterpillar signals the end of this stage of its life cycle by hanging upside down from the top of its shelter in a distinctive J-shape. It molts one last time and is transformed into a shining chrysalis. Students observe and draw the chrysalis and speculate on what is happening to their caterpillars.

Lessons 9, 10, 11, and 12 focus on the adult stage of the life cycle, the beautiful butterfly. As the butterfly emerges, students observe the process and identify the butterfly body parts and learn how they function. For the next few days, students provide a variety of food for the butterflies and observe the specialized sucking mouth, the proboscis, in action. Then, after several days, the children release the butterflies, with the realization that butterflies are part of the natural world.

In the final three lessons, students refine their understanding of the butterfly as an insect and of the life-cycle concept. First, they review their own data and observations of the life cycle of the Painted Lady. Then they relate to other living things what they have learned about butterflies.

The **Appendices** contain important information, including post-unit assessments of student progress, read-aloud stories about the discovery and history of silk, information on how to construct free or low-cost butterfly flight cages, and information about raising a second generation of butterflies. Also included is an annotated bibliography of books that contains references for teachers and students, examples of children's literature, and general sources of information about life cycles.

Materials List

Below is a list of the materials needed for *The Life Cycle of Butterflies* unit. Please note that the metric and English equivalent measurements in this unit are approximate.

1 *The Life Cycle of Butterflies* Teacher's Guide

*30 optional Student Notebooks (*My Butterfly Book*)

1 class calendar

*30 Painted Lady butterfly caterpillars

*1 container of caterpillar food, 236 ml (8 oz)

30 clear plastic cups, 30 ml (1 oz), with lids and tissues

1 spoon

1 paintbrush

2 large butterfly cages

30 hand lenses

4 feeding stations consisting of:
  sugar
  sponge pieces
  petri dishes or shallow jar lids

4 paper cups

** Supplies for making caterpillar models (see Lesson 4)

** Twigs for butterfly cages

** Paper towels

** Masking tape

** Egg cartons

** Narrow-neck bottles

** Lined paper

** Drawing paper

** Crayons

** Newsprint

** Markers

** Double-sided tape

** Transparency

*Note: The optional Student Notebooks (in English or Spanish) are available from Carolina Biological Supply Company (800-334-5551). To receive the caterpillars and their food, mail in the prepaid order card enclosed in the kit box. See page 5 for more information on ordering.

**Note: These items are not included in the kit. They are available in most schools or can be brought from home.

Important Information about Releasing Butterflies

The National Science Resources Center (NSRC) has decided to advise against the release of any organism used in the Science and Technology for Children™ program. In some documented cases, environmental problems have resulted from the introduction of nonindigenous organisms. It is also illegal in many states to release organisms, even indigenous species, without a permit. The intention of these laws is protection of native wildlife and the environment. If you have questions about releasing organisms in your area, contact your state or local environmental conservation agency.

Lesson 12 of *The Life Cycle of Butterflies* calls for students to release the Painted Lady butterflies they have been observing during the unit. The NSRC advises you not to release the butterflies. As an alternative, the NSRC recommends that you build a flight cage and raise a second generation of butterflies (see Appendix C and Appendix D, pgs. 105-107). Students can then observe the butterflies through the completion of their life cycle. When the butterflies die, you may wish to mount them for a display.

The Painted Lady butterfly (*Vanessa cardui*) was thoroughly researched before it was selected for *The Life Cycle of Butterflies.* It supports the goals of the unit, it is easy to use in the classroom, and it is available year-round. The butterfly also can be cultured (or raised); therefore, the population in the wild is not depleted. Commonly found throughout North America, Painted Lady butterflies probably would not harm native wildlife and local ecosystems if released. Release of the butterflies, however, might encourage your students to release other organisms that could do harm.

The Life Cycle of the Painted Lady Butterfly*

Sunday	Monday	Tuesday	Wednesday	Thursday	Friday	Saturday
		EGG (3 to 5 Days)				CATERPILLAR····
····		CATERPILLAR (12 to 18 Days)				····
····		CATERPILLAR				····
····CATERPILLAR···			··· ADULT BUTTERFLY		CHRYSALIS (7 to 10 Days)····	
·· CHRYSALIS			(2 Weeks) ···			···

*Sample Class Calendar

Teaching Strategies and Classroom Management Tips

The teaching strategies and classroom management tips in this section will help you give students the guidance they need to make the most of the hands-on experiences in this unit. These strategies and tips are based on the assumption that students already have formed many ideas about how the world works and that useful learning results when they have the opportunity to re-evaluate their ideas as they engage in new experiences and encounter the ideas of others.

Classroom Discussion: Class discussions, effectively led by the teacher, are important vehicles for science learning. Research shows that the way questions are asked, as well as the time allowed for responses, can contribute to the quality of the discussion.

When you ask questions, think about what you want to achieve in the ensuing discussion. For example, open-ended questions, for which there is no one right answer, will encourage students to give creative and thoughtful answers. Other types of questions can be used to encourage students to see specific relationships and contrasts or to help them to summarize and draw conclusions. It is good practice to mix these questions. It also is good practice always to give students "wait-time" to answer. (Some researchers recommend a minimum of 3 seconds.) This will encourage broader participation and more thoughtful answers.

Brainstorming: A brainstorming session is a whole-class exercise in which students contribute their thoughts about a particular idea or problem. It can be a stimulating and productive exercise when used to introduce a new science topic. It also is a useful and efficient way for the teacher to find out what students know and think about a topic. As students learn the rules for brainstorming, they will become more and more adept in their participation.

To begin a session, define for students the topics about which ideas will be shared. Tell students the following rules:

- Accept all ideas without judgment.

- Do not criticize or make unnecessary comments about the contributions of others.

- Try to connect your ideas to the ideas of others.

***The Life Cycle of Butterflies* Student Notebook:** An option for this unit is a consumable notebook for students, *My Butterfly Book*. This notebook includes all the activity sheets used in the unit, as well as a limited number of pages for student drawings and writings.

If you have these notebooks, you will want to collect them periodically to assess student progress. At the conclusion of the unit, students may keep their notebooks as a reminder of all they have learned.

If you do not use these ready-made notebooks, be sure to duplicate for students the **Activity Sheets** found in the Teacher's Guide at the end of most lessons. Reminders of the need for Activity Sheet duplication are included in the **Preparation** sections of the appropriate lessons.

Ways to Group Students: One of the best ways to teach hands-on science lessons is to arrange students in small groups of two to four. There are several advantages to this organization. It offers pupils a chance to learn from one another by sharing ideas, discoveries, and skills, and, with coaching, students can develop important, interpersonal skills that will serve them well in all aspects of life. Finally, by having children help each other in groups, you will have more time to work with those students who need the most help.

As students work, often it will be productive for them to talk about what they are doing, resulting in a steady hum of conversation. If you or others in the school are accustomed to a quiet room, this new, busy atmosphere may require some adjustment. It will be important, of course, to establish some limits to keep the noise under control.

Planning Ahead: Being prepared is the key to success with this unit. Please read the general management tips given below, and watch for additional tips scattered throughout the unit where you see this icon:

- Order the caterpillars and caterpillar food. If you are using *The Life Cycle of Butterflies* kit of materials from Carolina Biological, send in the prepaid order card for living materials at least 20 days before beginning Lesson 2. If not, be sure to contact your supplier of living organisms for a delivery schedule.

- Enlist the help of another adult, especially for Lessons 2, 7, and 12.

- Preview each lesson ahead of time. Familiarize yourself with the background information, and think about how to organize and distribute the materials for each lesson.

- Try to be flexible. Like all living things, butterflies are not completely predictable. The **Sample Class Calendar** on pg. 3 gives you a sample timetable, but expect deviations, and be prepared for unexpected interruptions if students observe an exciting event taking place. This **Sample Class Calendar** also gives you an idea of the kinds of observations you and the class will be recording on the large **Class Calendar**.

- Plan for several short (15-minute) field trips on the school grounds for the following activities:
  –looking for caterpillar food plants
  –picking flowers to place in the butterfly cages

  –collecting twigs to place in the cages
  –finding the best place to release the butterflies
  –looking for evidence of other life cycles

- Consider letting interested children build their own butterfly cages. See **Appendix C** for ideas.

Setting up a Learning Center: Supplemental science materials should be given a permanent home in the classroom in a spot designated as the learning center. Such a center could be used by students in a number of ways: as an "on your own" project center, as an observation post, as a trade book reading nook, or simply as a place to spend unscheduled time when assignments are done.

In order to keep interest in the center high, change it or add to it often. Here are a few suggestions of items to include:

- Science trade books on plants and insects

- Magnifying glasses and an assortment of interesting objects to observe, such as leaves, seeds, stems, roots, flowers, insects, and soil and rocks from the playground, newspaper, fabric scraps, sponges, chalk, salt, and feathers

- Audiovisual materials on related subjects, such as plants, insects, life cycles, or famous scientists

- Items contributed by students for sharing, such as an insect collection, a honeycomb, magazine or newspaper articles, pictures, books, and model animals

Curriculum Integration: There are many opportunities for curriculum integration in this unit. Look for the following icons for math, reading, writing, art, speaking, and social studies that highlight these opportunities.

Evaluation: In the STC project, evaluation tools are included throughout each unit, and post-unit assessments are provided at the end. This arrangement is intended to help you assess what students know and monitor how they are progressing, making it easier for you to provide assistance to students who need it, to go over materials students did not grasp, and to report to parents on student progress. The assessments provided also are intended to be directly helpful to students, giving them an opportunity to reflect on their own learning, gain confidence by viewing their own progress, articulate the ways in which they want and need to grow, and formulate further questions.

Evaluation Preparation: To facilitate successful documentation and assessment of students' learning in the specific content areas of a unit as well as in the development of relevant skills, you should be prepared to:

- **Collect pre/post information.** One of the best indicators of student learning comes through gathering information from an identical activity or discussion conducted both before and after a unit. The pre-test suggested for use in Lesson 1 of this unit is also a suggested post-test. Note that comparison of non-identical materials generated early and late in a unit also can help you gauge growth in learning. You will want to make sure that pretest and post-test work is dated.

- **Encourage students to use notebooks—those supplied to them or their own—in a way that is useful to you and to them.** Student notebooks provide information about student progress. To ensure that you will be able to make the best use of these notebooks, be sure to ask students to:

  - make only one entry per page;
  - date each entry;
  - write out conclusions and interpretations of experiments;

  - write explanations to charts, tables, and graphs; and
  - include the question when writing out answers.

  Student notebooks are a particularly handy and effective way to share student progress and accomplishments with parents and other interested adults as well as with the students themselves.

- **Observe.** Invaluable for assessment are your ongoing observations of students as they work, written in your notebook or on file cards.

- **Allow time for oral presentations.** Oral presentations by students can be useful vehicles for assessment.

A variety of post-unit assessment instruments is offered in **Appendix A**. From those suggested, you will want to choose only the instruments that are most appropriate for measuring the achievement level of your class. Consider using more than one, in order to give students with differing learning styles a chance to express their knowledge and skills. Different styles of assessment have been shown to be particularly helpful in increasing the precision of the assessment of girls and minorities—two groups that have historically underperformed in science.

Please note that **Appendix A** includes a black line master for a "Teacher's Record Chart of Student Progress." You may want to reproduce this chart at the beginning of the unit to help you record individual student achievement throughout the unit. Please remember that most students at the grade level targeted by this unit will not be able to master and articulate the full list of skills.

LESSON 1

Getting Ready for Caterpillars

Overview

Over the next few weeks, your class will observe the life cycle of a Painted Lady butterfly. Students will watch their own caterpillar grow, shed its skin several times, transform into a chrysalis (KRISS-uh-liss), and emerge as a black and orange butterfly—all within less than a month.

Today, you will prepare your students for the arrival of these special creatures in your classroom. You also will assess what students already know about the relationship between caterpillars and butterflies.

Objectives

- Students look forward to the arrival of the caterpillars.
- Students express in words and drawings what they already know about caterpillars and butterflies for evaluation by the teacher.

Background

The Painted Lady butterfly (scientific name *Vanessa cardui*) has several characteristics that make it ideal for classroom use. It is the most widely distributed of all butterflies, it will eat and thrive on a commercially prepared food, and its development is rapid.

Because the Painted Lady butterfly is found at some time of year on every continent except South America and Antarctica, this species also is called the "Cosmopolitan butterfly." During yearly spring migrations, the butterflies move from warm tropical areas northward to the Arctic Circle and southward to the limits of the continents. The thousands of Painted Lady butterflies that flit across North America each spring have migrated from Mexico or Southern California. In the fall, the survivors will go South for the warm winter.

The common plant foods of the Painted Lady caterpillars include many that are considered weeds, such as mallow, thistle, plantain, and dandelion. The Painted Ladies you and your students will raise are easily maintained in the classroom when fed with a commercially prepared food. It is a mixture of plant materials plus vitamins and minerals. In the next lesson, you will learn more about the diet of the Painted Lady caterpillars and the possibility of gathering natural foods for them to eat.

Figure 1-1

Range map of the Painted Lady butterfly

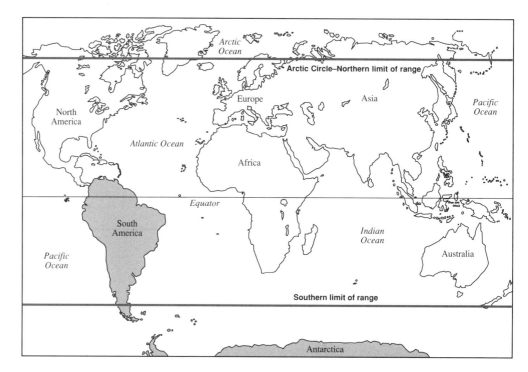

During the course of this unit, you and the children will witness one of the marvels of nature, **metamorphosis** (meht-uh-MOR-fuh-sihs). Metamorphosis is defined as marked developmental changes in the form or structure of an animal as it matures. This means that the body of the young is completely different from the body of the adult. The butterfly goes through what is known as **complete metamorphosis**, a life cycle consisting of four distinct stages. These stages are:

- The egg. The egg of the Painted Lady is tiny and blue-green in color. The adult butterfly lays about 500 eggs at a time that hatch into caterpillars 3 to 5 days later.

- The caterpillar. Sometimes called the larva, the caterpillar lives to eat. This stage lasts from 12 to 18 days; during this time, the caterpillar grows very rapidly and sheds its nongrowing outer skin five times to accommodate its increasing size.

- The chrysalis (KRISS-uh-liss). Also called the pupa (PYOO-puh), this is a time when the animal goes through its most remarkable changes. Hanging nearly motionless and encased in a shiny hard covering for about one week, the animal emerges as a butterfly.

- The butterfly. The winged adult lives for about 2 weeks. It mates on the second or third day after it emerges, and the female lays eggs for several days thereafter, thus ensuring the continuation of the cycle.

Figure 1-2 shows the life cycle of the Painted Lady and the approximate number of days in each stage of the cycle.

Full-page illustrations of each of these stages of development are provided in **Appendix F**, beginning on pg. 113. You may find photocopies of these useful as bulletin board materials or as masters for overhead transparencies.

The time required for each developmental stage varies with the temperature. Development from larva to adult may take place as quickly as 19 days in

Figure 1-2

*The life cycle of
the Painted Lady
butterfly*

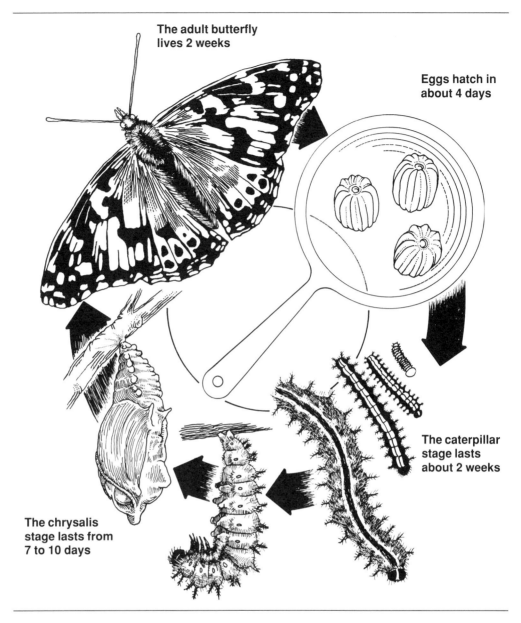

The adult butterfly
lives 2 weeks

Eggs hatch in
about 4 days

The caterpillar
stage lasts
about 2 weeks

The chrysalis
stage lasts from
7 to 10 days

warm weather or as long as 28 days in cool weather. You will have the same situation in your classroom. If room temperatures are exceptionally warm, development will be fast. If room temperatures are cool, the development of the insects will be slowed.

Materials

For each student

    1   sheet of drawing paper

    1   sheet of lined paper

For the teacher

    2   large sheets of newsprint and markers

        OR

    2   overhead transparencies and markers with a projector

Preparation

1. Let the school office know that you are expecting a package containing live caterpillars so they will inform you immediately when it arrives.

2. Obtain the materials to record student ideas during the brainstorming session. Label one sheet "What we know about caterpillars." Label the second sheet "What we would like to find out about caterpillars."

   Note: If your class is using *The Life Cycle of Butterflies* Student Notebook, they will not need the drawing and writing paper specified for each student. In future lessons, you will not need to duplicate the **Activity Sheets**, as they are in the notebook.

Procedure

1. Announce to the class that some caterpillars are coming to live in the classroom for a while. The class will watch them grow and change. When the caterpillars have become butterflies, you will set them free outdoors, where they belong.

2. Now, conduct a brainstorming session with the students to find out what they already know about caterpillars. Here are some guidelines for brainstorming. Discuss them with your students.

   - Accept all ideas without judgment.

   - Do not criticize or make unnecessary comments about the contributions of others.

   - Try to connect your ideas to the ideas of others.

3. Display the chart entitled "What we know about caterpillars." Use it to record all student responses as objectively as possible. You may wish to use some of the following questions to help focus the discussion:

   - What are caterpillars?

   - What do they look like?

   - Where have you seen caterpillars?

   - What were they doing?

   - What happens to caterpillars? What do caterpillars look like when they are grown?

4. Display the second chart entitled "What we would like to find out about caterpillars." Use it to record student questions.

5. Keep both charts. They will be useful as:

   - Pre-unit assessments. Through discussion and the asking of questions, students have shared important information about what they know about caterpillars and butterflies. Now you can build on their knowledge and experiences. As you teach each lesson, have students add new ideas to the list. Write the new information with a different colored pen.

   - Post-unit assessments. When you have completed the unit, display the lists of the class's ideas as they have developed over time. Let students review the lists to evaluate their own progress. See **Appendix A** for details.

6. Distribute pencils and paper. Ask students to:

- Draw a picture of what they think a caterpillar looks like.

- Show in drawings how a caterpillar changes during its life. These drawings and/or writings will be useful in later assessments of student learning.

   Note: It is important that a drawing of a butterfly be included in the students' illustrations. If students don't include it spontaneously, prompt them to do so.

Final Activities

Collect the drawings and keep them out of sight until the post-unit assessment. Tell students that at the end of the unit they will do another drawing of the life of a caterpillar. Then they will hang the two drawings side by side to assess for themselves how much they have learned.

Extensions

1. The **Bibliography** lists many excellent trade books about caterpillars. Select one to read aloud to the class.

2. If you have set up a science learning center, direct students to the hand lenses and encourage students to begin using them. See Lesson 2, pg. 17, for instructions on how to use the hand lens correctly. This individual practice will help prepare students for the close observations of the caterpillars they will be performing in Lesson 2.

3. For a creative writing exercise, try this topic: "Some caterpillars are coming. What problems might they have living in our classroom?"

Evaluation

During the course of the unit, children will create drawings and complete **Activity Sheets** that you can use as an evaluation tool. These **Activity Sheets** are available in *The Life Cycle of Butterflies* Student Notebook, which children may write in and take home after the unit has been completed. Alternatively, you may supply paper and activity sheets for the children to use and keep in their own notebooks.

The children's first drawings and descriptions of a caterpillar will serve as a "before" picture to be used as a comparison with drawings made during and after the completion of the unit. As you examine these first drawings, look for details in body structure. Do the students recognize a head, legs, body segments, or other details of caterpillars and butterflies they may have seen in the past? Use these drawings to help you determine which new structures or details the students begin to notice as they make observations.

It will be useful to note, too, how much students understand about the relationship between caterpillars and butterflies and how much they already know about the life cycle.

- The caterpillars are usually between 3 and 6 days old when they arrive in your classroom, and they already have undergone at least two molts. Because it is important for the students to observe and describe the earliest stages of the caterpillars, try to teach the next lesson—Lesson 2—on the day the caterpillars arrive.

■ If you must delay beginning the unit, you may put the caterpillars in the vegetable bin of a refrigerator at 40° to 50°F for up to one week. This will retard caterpillar growth.

> **WARNING:** Keeping caterpillars colder than 40°F for more than one week jeopardizes both caterpillar and butterfly health, increasing the chances that the butterflies will emerge deformed.

■ For Lesson 2, try to recruit an adult or upper-grade students to help you manage the distribution of food cups and caterpillars. See the **Preparation** section in Lesson 2, pg. 16, for details.

Draw a picture of what you think a caterpillar looks like.

Draw pictures to show how a caterpillar changes during its life.

LESSON 2

Caring for Caterpillars

Overview

Today the caterpillars arrive. Students prepare the food cups vital to the survival of the caterpillars and learn how to care for them. Then students meet the caterpillars and record their first observations.

Objectives

■ Students prepare the food cups and learn how to care for the caterpillars.

■ Students learn how to use a magnifier.

■ Students make and record their first observations of the caterpillars.

Background

The commercial food for these caterpillars is processed from plants they would eat in the wild. These plants belong to the Mallow family (Malvaceae). One member of the family that Painted Lady butterflies prefer is the round-leaved mallow, or *Malva neglecta*.

Malva neglecta is a sprawling plant that grows to a height of about 2 feet. Its rounded or heart-shaped leaves with scalloped edges are where the female butterfly chooses to lay her eggs. When the hatchling caterpillars emerge, they have ready access to a food supply.

Figure 2-1

Malva neglecta,
or the round-leaved mallow

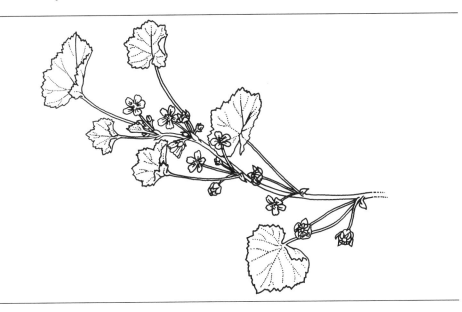

The *Malva neglecta* is a hardy plant that blooms from May through October. Its five-petaled white or pale-lavender flowers can be seen peeking out of relatively dry weedy areas.

Do not allow children to handle caterpillars. They are delicate and easily crushed. Also, acids in perspiration on human fingertips may hamper the molting process.

Materials

For each student
- 1   1-ounce cup with lid and tissue
- 1   teaspoon of caterpillar food
- 1   **Activity Sheet 1, Caterpillar Food** (if your students do not have individual copies of *My Butterfly Book* Student Notebook)
- 1   hand lens

For the class
   Class Calendar

For the teacher
- 1   paintbrush
- 1   spoon
- 3   egg cartons or storage trays
- 1   8 oz. container of caterpillar food
- 1   container of caterpillars
- 1   terrarium and lid (optional)

Preparation

1.   When you receive your caterpillar shipment, you also should receive enough food to raise the caterpillars. The caterpillars and the food need to be divided among a class set of small cups with lids. A soft paintbrush will be helpful in transferring the caterpillars.

2.   Prepare the individual caterpillar cups by:

   ■   Placing one teaspoon of caterpillar food in each cup

   ■   Labeling each lid with each student's name

   Do not pack the food down. The students will do this.

3.   Reproduce **Activity Sheet 1**, if necessary

4.   Post the **Class Calendar** on the bulletin board. You will be using it to record observations for the class.

5.   Make arrangements for assistants to help you with the distribution of cups, lids and tissues, and caterpillars.

6.   Have students wash their hands with soap and water before touching the food.

Procedure

1. Introduce the lesson by discussing the caterpillars' foods with the class. Talk about their natural food as well as the prepared food supplied in the cups.

2. Tell students that they will prepare the cups of food for the caterpillars by packing the food down in the cups. Explain that this is a very important step because loose food can shift and crush the caterpillars.

3. Distribute one cup with food and one lid to each child. With clean fingers, the children should now push the food firmly into the bottoms of the cups. Ask them to try not to smear the food on the sides of the cups because this will make it more difficult to see the caterpillars inside later on.

4. As the children work, ask them what they observe about the food using each of the senses except taste. (The caterpillar food is not toxic, but it is good practice not to taste anything in science class.) Encourage the children to talk about the color, texture, and odor of the food.

5. Next, show students two ways to use the hand lenses to look at the food in the cups, as demonstrated in Figure 2-2.

Figure 2-2

Two ways to use a hand lens

- ■ Place the lens close to your eye, where a lens would be if you were wearing glasses. Hold the object in your other hand and move it back and forth slowly until it is in focus.

- ■ Or, hold the object stationary, with the hand lens above the object. Now move the magnifier back and forth to focus.

6. Distribute the hand lenses and allow students time to practice with them. Before distributing the caterpillars, stress the fact that caterpillars are very delicate and must be handled gently. Caution students never to hold the cups upside down.

7. To distribute the caterpillars, use a small paintbrush to transfer them one by one from the large cup to each of the student containers. As soon as students receive their caterpillars, they should place a tissue over the open cup and snap the lid on the cup. Remove the excess tissue from around the rim. The caterpillar attaches to the tissue to form the chrysalis.

   Allow students time to use the hand lenses to observe the caterpillars and the food.

8. After students have had time to observe, pass out **Activity Sheet 1** (or the Student Notebook) and preview it with the class. It is important to include the date today. You will need the date again in Lesson 13. Give students sufficient time to complete **Activity Sheet 1**.

9. At the end of the lesson, collect the caterpillar cups for storage in the egg cartons until the next lesson. Or, use double-sided tape to attach the cups to the student desk tops so that they can observe the caterpillars throughout the day.

Final Activities

1. Ask students to share what they have observed about the caterpillars. Have the class dictate a description of the caterpillars to record on the **Class Calendar**. Then, draw a box around this date on the calendar. You will need this information again in Lesson 13 to complete **Activity Sheet 11**.

2. Briefly discuss what the children think the caterpillars will look like tomorrow. You may wish to record their predictions to review after they observe the caterpillars tomorrow.

Extensions

1. There probably will be a few extra caterpillars in your shipment. You may wish to use these extras to set up a terrarium for your learning center. A terrarium offers some distinct advantages. Because it is so large, the terrarium permits students to observe more caterpillar activities. As caterpillars crawl along the side of the terrarium, it also is possible for students to make crude measurements of size. Students may lay a small piece of paper, string, or pipe cleaner along the outside of the terrarium and mark the length of the caterpillar. Students also have the opportunity to observe the caterpillars consuming food in a somewhat more natural environment. If you do construct a terrarium, you will need to provide the food for the caterpillars. See No. 2 below. Remember, caterpillars are voracious eaters, so don't undertake this project if adequate food is not available.

2. The foods that caterpillars like best are all in the Mallow family. You may even have them in your schoolyard: rose of Sharon (*Hibiscus syriacus*), hollyhock (*Althaea rosea*), or marsh mallow (*Althaea officinalis*). Other plants that the caterpillars may eat include the leaves of thistle, nettle, sage, plantain, and dandelion. If possible, take a short field trip outdoors to collect some of these natural foods.

> **Safety Reminder**
>
> Some thistles have sharp spines and some nettles have stinging hairs.
> Exercise caution when gathering these plants.

3. Watch for the development of mold in the terrarium, particularly on the
    food sources you bring in from outdoors. Replace wilted leaves daily. If a
    small caterpillar is feeding on a leaf that needs to be removed, use
    scissors to clip around the caterpillar or move it gently with a paintbrush.

    Figure 2-3 shows a completed caterpillar terrarium.

Figure 2-3

*A completed
caterpillar terrarium*

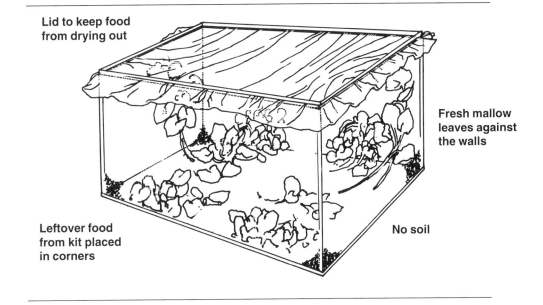

Lid to keep food
from drying out

Fresh mallow
leaves against
the walls

Leftover food
from kit placed
in corners

No soil

Caterpillar Food   **Activity Sheet 1**

Name: _____

_____

Write the date the caterpillars arrived: [   ]

Look closely at the caterpillar's food. Then answer the questions below.

How does the food feel?
_____
_____

How does the food smell?
_____
_____

How does the food look?
_____
_____

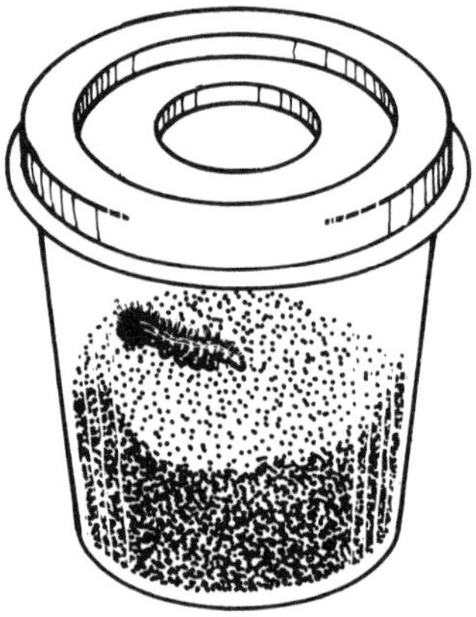

Activity Sheet 1

The food is made from a plant called mallow.
This is a mallow plant. It has green leaves and light purple
flowers. You can color the mallow plant.

Learning More about Caterpillars

Overview

Now that the caterpillars have arrived in your classroom, it is up to you and your students to provide for their basic needs—food, water, shelter, and air. In this lesson, students observe the caterpillars and learn more about how to take care of them.

Objectives

- Students learn about the characteristics that living things share.

- Students become aware of what living things need to survive.

- Students recognize the specific needs of their caterpillars.

- Students observe how caterpillars grow and change.

Background

For caterpillars to remain healthy in an artificial environment, such as the classroom, they must be provided with food, water, shelter, and air. Complicating matters are the caterpillar's poor eyesight and small brain. If food is not underfoot, caterpillars may starve as they roam in circles looking for something to eat.

Caterpillars are much more selective about their food than we are. We eat a variety of different foods, but caterpillars will eat only a limited number of plants. As mentioned in Lesson 2, the Mallow family of plants (Malvaceae) is the preferred source of food for the Painted Lady caterpillars. The commercial food in the kit is made from plants of the genus *Malva* and provides additional nourishment in the form of vitamin and mineral additives. The moisture in the food provides all the water the caterpillars need.

A caterpillar needs shelter, too. In nature, it would pitch a tent above its head by spinning strands of silk across leaves to make a roof-like shelter, as shown in Figure 3-1. In the classroom, the cup is a convenient shelter for the caterpillars.

While caterpillars can tolerate a fairly wide range of temperatures, they should not be placed in direct sunlight because temperatures in the cup can rise quickly. Also, direct sunlight may cause water to evaporate from the moist food and condense on the sides of the cup. Caterpillars are so small that they can drown in a water drop!

Figure 3-1

*Caterpillar shelter as
it appears in the wild*

Finally, air is vital to caterpillars, as it is to most living things; without it, they cannot survive more than a few minutes. There is a hole in the lid of the cup to provide enough air until the caterpillars change into chrysalises and are moved to a new container.

Materials

For each student

    1 caterpillar in cup

    1 hand lens

    1 **Activity Sheet 2, Taking Care of My Caterpillar** (if students do not have *The Life Cycle of Butterflies* Student Notebook)

For the class

    Class Calendar

Preparation

Duplicate **Activity Sheet 2**, if needed.

Procedure

1. Begin with a short period of observation. Tell students that you want them to use their hand lenses to look at the caterpillars closely for signs that they are alive.

2. Open the discussion by asking "How do you know if something is alive?" Students may mention that living things move, eat, grow, respond, eliminate, and reproduce. Develop the idea that living things share some important characteristics.

3. Then go on to discuss the idea that every living creature needs certain things to stay alive. These basic needs include air, water, food, appropriate temperature, and shelter. Ask students if caterpillars and people have the same needs.

4. Finally, ask students to think about how the caterpillars receive each of these vital elements when they are in your classroom. (See the **Background** section for details.)

5. Distribute **Activity Sheet 2** or have students turn to it in their Student Notebooks. Preview the sheet with the class. Allow students sufficient time to complete the sheet.

Final Activities

1. Ask the children to dictate a statement for you to record on the **Class Calendar**. This statement should reflect what the students have observed about the caterpillars during this lesson.

2. Ask students what they think the caterpillars will look like tomorrow. Mention that this exercise is called making a prediction. A prediction is based on what has already been observed. It is not a wild guess.

3. Return the cups to the egg cartons for storage and either collect Student Notebooks or put activity sheets in the students' portfolios, whichever is appropriate.

Extensions

Have children think about the needs of other living things, such as plants that may be growing in the classroom, fish in aquariums, or favorite animals at the zoo.

Evaluation

Take note if any of your students are still having difficulty using the hand lenses. Offer them extra coaching and practice.

Taking Care of My Caterpillar   **Activity Sheet 2**

Name: _____

_____

Date: _____

_____

Take good care of your caterpillar.
Do not turn its cup upside down.
Do not drop your caterpillar.
Do not let the caterpillar get too hot or too cold.

Your caterpillar needs food, water, and air.

What does the caterpillar eat?

_____

_____

_____

_____

How does the caterpillar get water?

_____

_____

_____

_____

How does the caterpillar get air?

_____

_____

_____

_____

Observing the Caterpillars

Overview

Students began the unit by listing their questions about caterpillars. Today, they will seek answers to some of these questions by observing the caterpillars more closely.

Plan to teach Lessons 4, 5, and 6 during the second week that the caterpillars are in your classroom. These three lessons involve observing the caterpillar, with Lesson 5 emphasizing molting and Lesson 6 focusing on silk spinning. The sequence in which you teach these lessons depends in large part on the caterpillar structures or activities that are most in evidence that day.

Objectives

■ Students observe the structures and activities of caterpillars more closely.

■ Students predict what changes may occur next.

Background

A lot is happening inside the little cup. Over the next few days, the children will observe a wide range of activities and changes in the caterpillars. In the coming week, the caterpillars will grow rapidly, shed their skins—**molt**—several times, and become quietly encased as a pupa, or chrysalis.

Some general background necessary for teaching this lesson as well as the next two lessons is included in this section.

Caterpillar Body Parts

The caterpillar's head is covered by a dark, shiny capsule containing 12 small eyes, 6 on each side of the head. Although a butterfly has excellent eyesight, a caterpillar has simple eyes that can only distinguish between light and dark. Not all of the caterpillar's eyes are easily visible. Using a hand lens, students should be able to see some of them.

The chewing mouth is located on the underside of the head. The jaws do not chew up and down like ours; rather, they move back and forth from the sides of the head toward the middle. The eyes and mouth parts are most easily seen immediately after a molt, when the rest of the caterpillar body is pale and these structures are darker by comparison. It is likely that the children will not be able to see the eyes, mouth parts, or the silk spinners, which are located on the underside of the head, behind the mouth. Figure 4-1 shows an enlarged view of the silkworm caterpillar's head. The Painted Lady caterpillar's head is basically the same as this.

Figure 4-1

The caterpillar's head

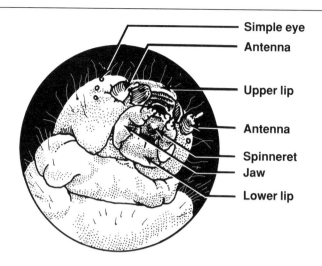

- Simple eye
- Antenna
- Upper lip
- Antenna
- Spinneret
- Jaw
- Lower lip

Behind the head, the caterpillar's body is divided into thirteen parts called **segments**. On each of the first three body segments, there is a pair of jointed legs, which will become the butterfly's long slender legs. These first three segments of the caterpillar's body will become the **thorax**, or midsection, of the adult insect.

Five segments toward the rear of the caterpillar have pairs of "false legs," also known as **prolegs**. The caterpillar does most of its walking on the fleshy prolegs, which act as suction cups when the insect crawls on a smooth surface. The prolegs are versatile. Across the bottom of each foot are rings of microscopic bristles shaped like crochet hooks. These hooks can cling to plant leaves and stems or to the threads of silk the caterpillar spins. The caterpillar uses the last pair of prolegs as an anchor when shedding its skin. All of these prolegs will disappear during the next stage of development, and the rear body segments will become the **abdomen**, or hind section of the adult.

The body is covered with **bristles** so that it reflects minimal light, making the body less visible to birds. The bristles also make it more difficult for a bird to swallow a caterpillar. Along each side of the body is a row of small breathing holes, called **spiracles** (SPEAR-uh-kuhls), which will be noticed by only the most observant. They appear as light-colored rings with dark centers. Fresh air is drawn in and stale air is expelled through these spiracles. A detailed drawing of the caterpillar with these body parts labeled is shown in Figure 4-2.

Growth and Molting (See Lesson 5 for more details)
Caterpillars spend a great deal of time eating. As food disappears from the cups, the children will begin to notice increased amounts of **frass**—little green pellets of waste eliminated by the caterpillars. The children also may see small, black, wrinkled wads in the cups. These are shed skins, the result of molting. If students are asking questions about these things, or if they actually observe a molt, feel free to move ahead to Lesson 5. You may return to Lesson 4 later.

Silk Spinning (See Lesson 6 for more details)
When a caterpillar sways its head back and forth in a rhythmic pattern, it is spinning silk. The silk threads are fine and may not be noticeable for the first few days. Each day, the caterpillars add silk to a bridge-like structure across

Figure 4-2

The caterpillar's body

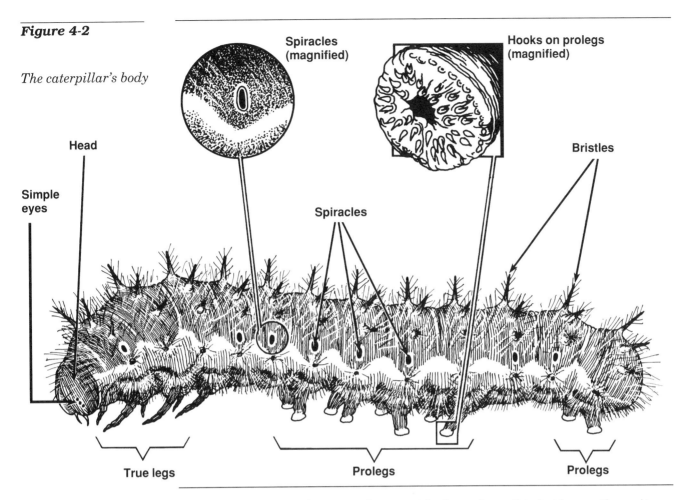

Spiracles
(magnified)

Hooks on prolegs
(magnified)

Head

Bristles

Simple
eyes

Spiracles

True legs

Prolegs

Prolegs

the top of the cup. They can cling upside-down from this bridge as they eat, rest, or molt. If children are asking questions about the rhythmic swaying motion or the silk itself, you may wish to teach Lesson 6 first and then come back to Lesson 4.

Materials

For each student

1   caterpillar in a cup
1   hand lens
1   **Activity Sheet 3, Observing the Caterpillar**

For the class

Photocopy or overhead of illustration of caterpillar from pg. 118
Newsprint pad or overhead transparency from Lesson 1
Overhead projector (if needed)
Class Calendar (on bulletin board)
Art materials for constructing caterpillar models (optional)

Preparation

1.   Spend a few minutes observing the caterpillars yourself to determine the order in which you want to teach the next three lessons.

2.   Hang on the bulletin board the illustration of the caterpillar on pg. 118, or reproduce it to use as an overhead transparency.

3. If you are going to construct any of the caterpillar models suggested in the **Extensions** section, collect the needed art materials.

Procedure

1. Begin the lesson by allowing students time to observe the caterpillars closely with the hand lenses. Tell them that the discussion today will be about the caterpillar's body parts and that they should try to learn as much as they can about their caterpillar's body.

2. During the observation period, circulate and help students focus by asking them specific questions. You might ask, for example,

    ■   What color is the caterpillar? How big is it? How would you describe its shape?

    ■   Which end is the head? How can you tell?

    ■   How many legs can you count?

    ■   Describe how the caterpillar moves. Can it walk on the smooth sides of the plastic cup? On the lid? On the food? On the silk?

    ■   What kind of body covering does it have?

    As the children observe, encourage them to talk with each other about what they are seeing. A student with a caterpillar that is resting should compare observations with someone watching an active caterpillar.

3. Ask children to put their caterpillars aside for a moment. Hold a class discussion about what they have learned by observing their caterpillars. You may use the illustration on pg. 118 either on the bulletin board or as an overhead projection to help focus the discussion. At the end of the discussion, return to the list of questions that students generated in Lesson 1 and have students note which ones they have answered through their observations.

4. Distribute **Activity Sheet 3** and preview it with the class. Allow sufficient time for students to complete the sheet.

Final Activities

1. Ask students to dictate statements for you to record on the **Class Calendar** on their observations about the caterpillar's body during this lesson.

2. Invite students to make predictions about how the caterpillars may be different by tomorrow.

3. Collect the caterpillar cups and return them to the storage place. Collect Student Notebooks or student work.

Extensions

Students can learn a great deal about caterpillar anatomy by constructing caterpillar models. Encourage them to create their own models based on what they have observed.

One idea to keep in mind is that a caterpillar can bend and turn because its body is made up of thirteen segments plus a head. This gives you a basic body plan to work from. Here are a few ideas of how to make models based on that plan:

■   Make a paper chain caterpillar of thirteen links plus a round disk for the head.

- Cut apart egg cartons for the body sections and head. Join the sections together with yarn or pipe cleaners.

- String cut-up soda straws, beads, noodles, gumdrops, or marshmallows together for the body segments and head. The last two suggestions are illustrated below.

Children can add details such as antennas, bristles, legs, spiracles and eyes for more interest.

Figure 4-3

Caterpillar models

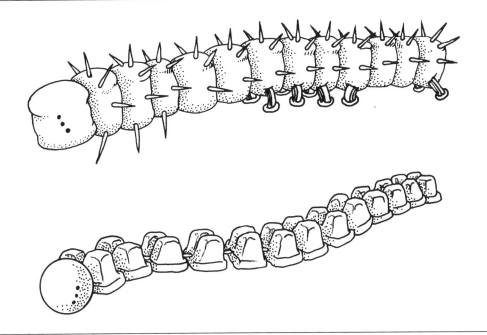

Observing My Caterpillar   **Activity Sheet 3**

Name:

Date:

A caterpillar has many parts. Each part helps the caterpillar.

The special legs help it move and hold onto leaves.

The special mouth is perfect for eating leaves.

The bristles make it hard for a bird to swallow a caterpillar.

Can you label the caterpillar? Look at the number next to each part. Then put the correct number in each box.

1. Two kinds of legs

2. Head

3. Eyes

4. Mouth

5. Bristles

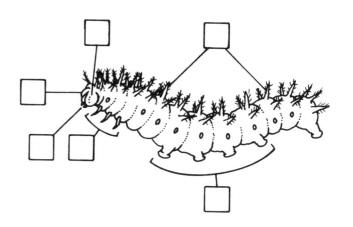

Write the letter of the caterpillar part next to what the part does.

A. Mouth   ___ Keep birds from eating it

B. Eyes   ___ Chews food and spins silk

C. Bristles   ___ Look for food

D. Legs   ___ Help the caterpillar move

Observing Change: Growth and Molting

Overview

During this lesson, students will be watching closely for the caterpillars to molt. Two to four molts may occur while the caterpillars are in your classroom, and if you and the children are lucky, you will witness a molt. Even if you don't, you still will see evidence that a molt has occurred.

Objectives

- Students observe growth and change in the caterpillars and relate this to changes in their own bodies.

- Students notice evidence of changes, such as shed skin, the shed head capsule, or increases in frass and decreases in food.

Background

Caterpillars eat large amounts of food and grow rapidly but because their skin is actually a rigid external skeleton, called an **exoskeleton**, they cannot increase in size without shedding the exoskeleton. All insects have an exoskeleton. As they consume food, their soft bodies grow inside their rigid exoskeleton, eventually filling up the available space. Molting is the term for the time when the insect sheds the exoskeleton and grows a new one.

Shortly before a molt, the caterpillar stops eating and becomes very still. Soon its body begins to pulse and seems to shorten and thicken. Then, much like the splitting of a seam in tight clothing, the exoskeleton near the caterpillar's head splits, and the soft insect inside wiggles out of its old exoskeleton. The last piece of exoskeleton to be shed is the head capsule. The illustrations in Figure 5-1 show a caterpillar molting.

You will be able to see evidence of the molt even if you do not witness the process. The discarded skin looks black and is in a wrinkled wad. The dark, shiny head capsule also will be lying in the cup. Sometimes this round head capsule is all you see because a caterpillar may eat all or part of the shed exoskeleton. It usually is possible to determine the number of molts that have occurred by counting the number of head capsules in the cup.

Immediately after a molt, the caterpillar's bristles and exoskeleton are extremely soft and pale. Now is the best time to see the eyes and mouth parts because they retain their dark color and contrast sharply with the body, which will soon darken and harden.

To increase the likelihood of watching a molt, you may wish to look through the cups and pick out caterpillars that have no shed skins (or a lesser

Figure 5-1

A caterpillar molting

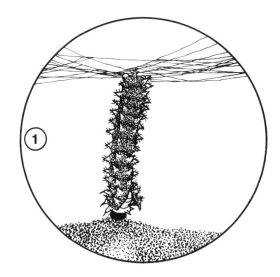

1. Skin splitting near the head.

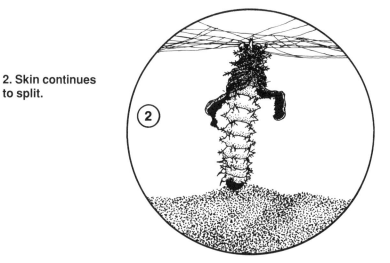

2. Skin continues to split.

3. Caterpillar after a molt. Head capsule and shed exoskeleton are at the bottom of the cup.

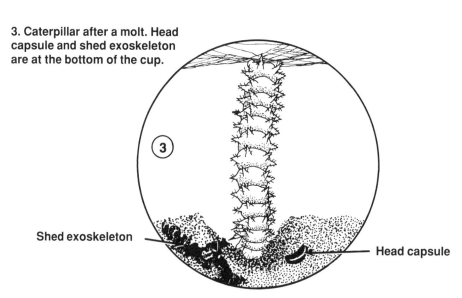

Shed exoskeleton

Head capsule

number of skins) and are exhibiting pre-molting behavior as described in the second paragraph of this section. You will have to watch the caterpillars closely. A molt happens in a matter of minutes.

Materials

For each student
1   caterpillar in a cup
1   hand lens
1   **Activity Sheet 4, My Caterpillar and Me**

For the class
   Class Calendar (on bulletin board)
   Caterpillar molting (illustration for bulletin board or overhead projector)

Preparation

1.   Examine the caterpillars. Look for shed skins or the typical behavior that precedes a molt. Make note of any caterpillars that may molt soon, so they can be observed frequently.

2.   Reproduce the illustration on pg. 119, either for the bulletin board or for an overhead projector.

Procedure

1.   The focus of this lesson is on how caterpillars grow and change. To spark discussion about the concept of growth and change, ask students how they have changed since they were in kindergarten. Can they wear the same shoes or clothes that they wore in kindergarten?

2.   Continue the discussion by asking children to reflect on their own growth and development since they were babies. The children will probably mention that their bodies are bigger, they have more hair and teeth, and they are larger and stronger now.

3.   Now, discuss the relationship between food and growth. Do students understand that food is responsible for their growth? Can students relate this concept to other animals, including caterpillars?

4.   Distribute caterpillars for the students to observe. Give the children an opportunity to observe how caterpillars are growing and to share discoveries with one another. Listen to the questions they ask. Keep a careful eye on any of the caterpillars that may be ready to molt so that you can seize the right moment to observe.

5.   To help students focus their observations, you may want to circulate around the class and ask some specific questions, such as:

   ■   What do you see in the cup that was not there the last time you looked?

   ■   Where do you think it came from?

   ■   What do you think it might be?

   ■   Does the caterpillar seem larger?

   Possible replies might include mention of frass, shed skins, or head capsules.

6. Put the caterpillars aside for a moment and hold a class discussion on the molting process. You may wish to use the illustration on pg. 119 as an overhead or as a bulletin board display.

7. Distribute the **Activity Sheet 4** and preview it with the class. Allow students time to complete the sheet.

Final Activities

1. Collect student booklets or **Activity Sheets** to be added to the portfolio.

2. Record observations on the **Class Calendar**.

3. If appropriate, revisit the list of questions students generated in Lesson 1 and answer any that pertain to the lesson today.

4. Although the children have seen that they are like the caterpillars in some ways, they also are very different. For example, a caterpillar's skin is not able to grow and stretch like a person's skin. To emphasize this point, play a game of "What if?" What if, when the students were babies, they were sewn inside their clothes so that they could not take them off. What would happen to the clothes as the children began to grow bigger and bigger? Ask children to use words and pictures to tell a story of what would happen in a situation like this.

Extensions

1. Read a story to the class about human growth and development. (See **Bibliography, Appendix E**.) You have already set the stage by asking the students to think about their own growth and development in the last 7 or 8 years. Help students relate the story to themselves in later years. Ask students to predict some things that will happen soon in their lives. Ask them to think about what might happen when they are teenagers and when they are grown-ups.

2. As a movement or dance exercise, ask children to dramatize how a caterpillar moves in order to shed its skin.

My Caterpillar and Me   **Activity Sheet 4**

Name: _____

_____

Date: _____

_____

In some ways, you are like your caterpillar.

In other ways, you are very different.

How many do you have?   How many of these does the caterpillar have?

___ Legs   ___ Legs
___ Eyes   ___ Eyes
___ Mouth   ___ Mouth
___ Head capsule   ___ Head capsule

When you grow, your skin grows with you.
A caterpillar's skin does not grow.
How does the caterpillar get bigger?

_____

_____

_____

_____

_____

_____

_____

Silk Spinning

Overview

Today students observe caterpillars' silk and try to discover caterpillars in the process of producing it. Students also learn why silk is important to caterpillars.

Objectives

■ Students observe and draw the silk threads spun by a caterpillar.

■ Students understand how a caterpillar uses silk.

Background

Most people may use silk only for special occasions, but a caterpillar uses its silk every day. The silk is spun from a specialized organ call a **spinneret**, located behind the mouth, as shown in Figure 6-1.

Figure 6-1

The caterpillar's head

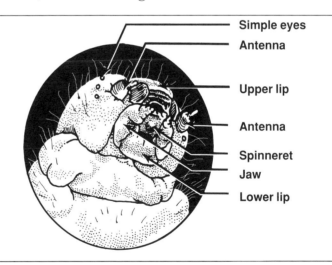

Simple eyes
Antenna
Upper lip
Antenna
Spinneret
Jaw
Lower lip

A modified salivary gland produces a thin stream of protein liquid that becomes a solid fiber as it passes through a tiny hole and comes into contact with the air. When a caterpillar waves its head from side to side, it is spinning a strong but nearly invisible strand of silk.

The caterpillar spins as it walks, often manipulating the silk thread with its front legs. It constructs silken ladders or bridges between leaves and stems and over surfaces upon which it crawls. The microscopic hooks on the prolegs cling to the silk strands for surefooted travel.

You and the students will observe a network of silk across the top of the caterpillar cups. In nature, the Painted Lady caterpillars would use this silk to lace leaves together, forming a tent. Safe inside, the caterpillar would munch on the walls, roof, and ceiling of its shelter.

However, in the cup, the caterpillar most frequently hangs upside down from the silk as it eats and rests. Also, when the caterpillar is ready to shed its exoskeleton, it will anchor its last pair of prolegs to the silk and then thrash its way out of its skin.

Within a few days, the caterpillars in your classroom will spin their last strands of silk into a sturdy button from which to hang while they are in the next stage in their life cycle, which is the pupa, or chrysalis. Once the insect's body is encased in the chrysalis, the spinneret and silk gland will disappear. The butterfly has no need for silk, and the substances in these caterpillar structures will reorganize and become butterfly parts.

Additional information about a special caterpillar known as a silkworm and human uses of silk is included in **Appendix B** on pg. 101. Also included is a Chinese legend about how silk was discovered.

Materials

For each student
- 1 caterpillar in a cup
- 1 hand lens
- 1 **Activity Sheet 5, A Caterpillar and Its Silk**

For the class
- **Class Calendar**

Preparation

1. Check to see that silk threads are visible in most if not all of the caterpillar cups.
2. Duplicate **Activity Sheet 5**, if necessary.

Procedure

1. Distribute caterpillars and hand lenses. Allow time for children to observe. Direct student attention to the silk. Ask students to concentrate on the amount of silk the caterpillar has spun and on its crisscross patterns. Then describe the typical head swaying motion of a caterpillar when spinning so students can look for it. Figure 6-2 shows a caterpillar spinning the silk.

Figure 6-2

A caterpillar spinning a fine network of silk

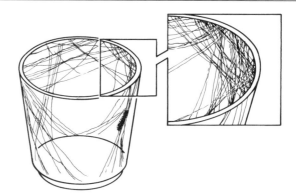

2. Distribute either the **Activity Sheet** or the Student Notebooks. Preview **Activity Sheet 5** with the class. Allow students time to complete it.

Final Activities

1. Conduct a discussion about what the children have observed. They may have seen caterpillars walking across the silk ladders or bridges, hanging from the silk as they ate or rested, as shown in Figure 6-3, or perhaps even securing themselves in preparation for a molt.

Figure 6-3

A caterpillar hanging from a silk thread

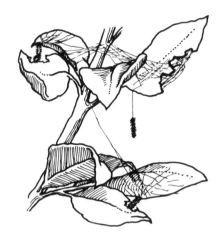

2. Some students may notice the caterpillars hanging in the distinctive "J-shape" that indicates they will soon become chrysalises. See Lesson 7 for more details about this stage. Can students see the thick silk button from which they hang? Ask students to predict what they think the caterpillars will look like the next time they are observed.

3. Collect the Student Notebooks or student work.

4. Ask the class to dictate a description of their most important observations for you to record on the **Class Calendar**.

Extensions

1. Does anyone in the class have silk clothing? We get silk from the silkworm, a moth larva that spins a silk cocoon. (Moths and butterflies are closely related, but one major difference is that during the pupal stage, moths spin a cocoon while butterflies form a chrysalis.) People have learned how to unravel the cocoons and use the threads to make fabrics. You can integrate science and social studies by learning about the production and use of silk fabric in Asia. See **Appendix B**, pg. 101, for a Chinese legend and a history of the silk industry.

2. Have the children seen other animals that use strands of silk? (Spiders, of course!) What are the similarities and differences in the ways caterpillars and spiders use silk?

If you plan to construct any of the optional flight cages suggested in **Appendix C**, pg. 105, begin the project soon. You will need to transfer the chrysalises to these cages within 2 or 3 days after they enter this stage.

A Caterpillar and Its Silk   **Activity Sheet 5**

Name: _____
_____

Date: _____
_____

When a caterpillar moves its head from side to side, it is spinning silk.

Look at the silk with a hand lens. See how the threads cross each other.

Draw a picture of the silken threads.

Why does a caterpillar need to spin silk?

_____
_____
_____
_____
_____
_____

From Caterpillar to Chrysalis

Overview

The caterpillar is about to undergo an amazing transformation. Soon it will turn into a chrysalis, the third stage in its life cycle. Students will observe the characteristic J-shape the caterpillar assumes before the transformation. Also, students may have the opportunity to witness the final molt that results in the chrysalis. A few days later, they will transfer the chrysalises to the butterfly flight cages.

Objectives

- Students observe the J-shape that precedes the caterpillar's transformation into a chrysalis.

- If possible, students witness the final molt that results in the chrysalis.

- The teacher assesses student progress in learning caterpillar anatomy and finds out how much students know about butterfly anatomy.

Background

The caterpillar is about to enter the third and most mysterious part of its life cycle. No one knows exactly how the next changes take place. Hidden within the thin shell of the chrysalis for about a week, the worm-like caterpillar body is changing into a graceful butterfly.

The six stumpy legs at the front of the caterpillar's body will become the long slender legs of the butterfly, and the prolegs will disappear. The leaf-chewing jaw will become a nectar-sucking organ called a **proboscis** (pro-BOSK-is). Four wings and the muscles to move them will develop. The insignificant lenses of the caterpillar's eyes will be replaced by hundreds of lenses in a compound eye, enabling the butterfly to see well enough to fly. These eyes also will seek a mate and then plants upon which to lay the fertilized eggs, because the adult butterfly's main job is to reproduce.

All of these dramatic changes are taking place inside a seemingly lifeless form. The chrysalis is not completely motionless, however, and you may observe it twitching from time to time. There are many excellent trade books illustrating the wide variety of chrysalis shapes, colors, and textures that conceal and protect the animal changing inside. (See the **Bibliography**, pg. 109.) The word "chrysalis" (plural: chrysalides or chrysalises) comes from the Greek word *chrysos*, which means gold. The Painted Lady chrysalis glistens with spots that are the color of this precious metal.

Another name given to this third stage in the life cycle is *pupa*. In Latin, pupa means doll. Many of these developing insects, especially the moths, do look like a baby in a blanket.

The Beginning of Pupation

Although the process of pupation is somewhat mysterious, the caterpillars will give you some clues that it is about to occur. When the caterpillars reach a length of 25 to 35 mm or about 1 to 1½ inches, watch for the following important signs. Also see Figure 7-1.

- The larvae stop eating and crawl to the lid of the cup.

- They spin a silk button on the lid.

- They hang head-down from the silk button in a characteristic J-shape. This means that chrysalises will form in a matter of hours.

Figure 7-1

From caterpillar to chrysalis

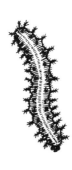  

A. Caterpillar at 25 to 35 mm (1 to 1½ inches)

B. Caterpillar hanging in a J-shape from a silk button

C. Chrysalis

Materials

For each student

1   caterpillar or chrysalis in cup
1   hand lens
1   **Activity Sheet 6, What Happens to the Caterpillar?**

For the class

2   butterfly flight cages
    Twigs
    Paper towels
    Class Calendar

Note: See **Appendix C** for ideas about how to construct free or low-cost butterfly cages.

Preparation

1.   Two or three days after the transformation, you will need to move the chrysalises into the butterfly flight cages that you have prepared. Here is a brief summary of several types of cages you might use:

- Two commercially made butterfly flight cages are included in the unit. Assemble them according to the directions provided in Figure 7-2. Two of these cages will provide enough space for all of the butterflies.

Figure 7-2

*Assembling a
flight cage*

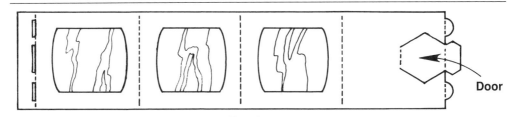

Panels

**Solid lines are die-cut; broken lines
are scored for folding. Note that
base and lid are identical except for
window in lid.**

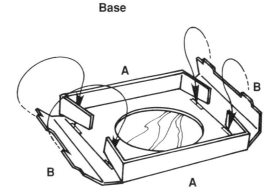

Door

**1. Fold panels inward (cellophane
inside) and insert tabs into slots.**

Base

Lid

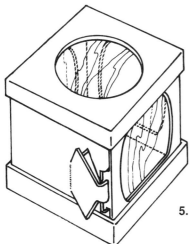

A

B

B

A

**2. Place lid face down
(cellophane on top).
Fold sides A up and
corners inward. Fold
sides B up and over
corners, and insert their
tabs into the slots.**

**3. Repeat Step 2 with
the base.**

**4. Fit the base and the lid
over the assembled panels.**

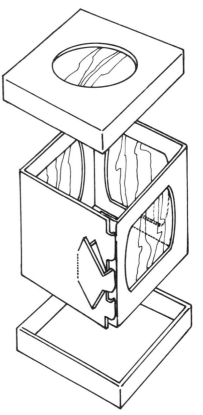

5. The cage is complete.

■ As an option, make free or low-cost cages from cardboard boxes or old lamp shades covered with nylon netting. Or construct a large hanging cage made of nylon netting. See **Appendix C**, pg. 105, for details.

2. No matter which kind of flight cages you use, you will need to line the bottom with paper towels to absorb the fluids the butterflies expel as they emerge. Also, the lining provides them with a foothold.

3. Add a few twigs to each cage for the butterflies to use as perches.

4. Duplicate **Activity Sheet 6.**

Procedure

1. Distribute the caterpillars and hand lenses. Allow time for observations. To help students focus on the changing caterpillar, ask them to notice the size of their caterpillars (about 25 to 35 mm, or 1 to 1½ inches), their level of activity (relatively inactive), whether or not they have spun a silk button on the lid of the cup, and their position in the cup (may be hanging in J-shape from lid).

   Chances are that you will find caterpillars in different stages of transformation, so allow children to observe one another's insects, too. There may be an opportunity for the class to witness a caterpillar going through its final molt and to see the chrysalis stage as it emerges from under the last exoskeleton.

2. Distribute **Activity Sheet 6**. Preview the **Activity Sheet** with the class and then give them time to complete it.

3. Hold a brief class discussion. Note that not all children will have the same observations because the caterpillars will transform over a period of several days. Discuss their different observations and add the important ones to the **Class Calendar**.

4. Draw a box around the date on your calendar to indicate when the first chrysalises form. You will need this information again in Lesson 13. Continue the discussion by asking why some caterpillars have not yet become chrysalises. (Like people, they are individuals and develop at their own pace.) Ask those who still have caterpillars to predict what their insects will look like tomorrow. Emphasize again that predictions are not wild guesses, but are based on reasons. What reasons can children give for their predictions?

Final Activities

1. After several days, the chrysalises that have dried and hardened are ready to be moved to their new flight cages . Be prepared to help children remove the lid from the cup. Caution them to treat each chrysalis very gently.

2. Put a small piece of double-sided tape on the top of the tissue. Show the children how to stick the tissue carefully on the side of the box—the closer to the bottom, the better. This way, if the chrysalises fall, they won't fall far.

3. If any chrysalises have become detached from the silk button, lay them gently on the paper towels near the side of the box. Then the butterflies can grasp the side of the box when they emerge. Be forewarned that the chrysalises that do not hang suspended may emerge with some deformity. If you set up the terrarium, you may wish to give the extra chrysalises in the terrarium to children who have one that is detached.

Extensions

1. Read a trade book to the students about the life cycle of another kind of living thing. See the **Bibliography**, pg. 109, for suggestions.

2. Practice making predictions. Have children suggest other situations where they could make predictions (weather, sports events, the lunch menu, which butterfly will emerge first). Ask students to give a reason for each prediction they make.

Evaluation

In Lesson 1, students made a drawing of a caterpillar. Now ask them to draw a caterpillar again. Ask them to label any parts they can. Both you and the children can compare these before and after drawings to see how much they have learned. Look for details such as a distinct head, eyes, bristles, body segments, true legs, and prolegs.

What Happens to the Caterpillar?   **Activity Sheet 6**

Name: _____

_____

Date: _____

Watch your caterpillar carefully when it gets to be this big.

The caterpillar will crawl to the top of the cup and spin a strong silk button.

Then it will hang upside down from the button. It will hang in a J-shape.

Draw your caterpillar
hanging in a J-shape.

Next, the skin splits along the caterpillar's back. After the last molt, you will see the chrysalis.

Soon the chrysalis will become hard. Then it is time for you to put your chrysalis in a new cage. Write the date when the chrysalis appeared:

Draw a caterpillar. Label all its parts.

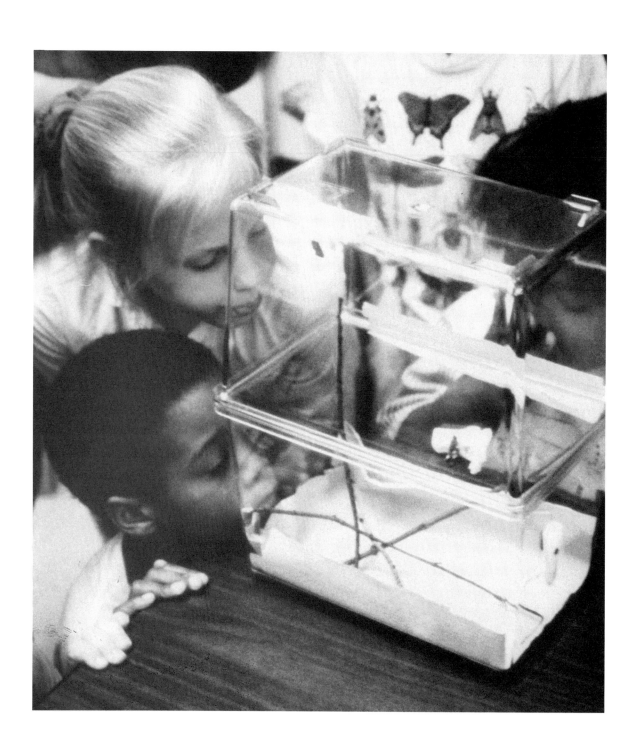

LESSON 8   Observing the Chrysalis

Overview

The chrysalis stage lasts for about 7 to 10 days. During this time, students will have several opportunities to make close observations.

Objectives

- Students work on their observational skills.

- Students realize that even at this apparently inactive stage, important changes are taking place within the chrysalis.

- Students make predictions about what will emerge from the chrysalis.

Background

Over the past few weeks, students have noticed dramatic changes in the caterpillars. This week, the changes students can observe will be subtle. Except for an occasional twitch, the pupa appears to be lifeless.

However, students will be able to see some of the butterfly structures that are forming under the protective shell. The pupa is hanging head-down. Two dark bulges are visible where the compound eyes are forming. Between the eyes, the shape of the long straw-like mouth, called the proboscis, is also visible. On either side of the mouth parts, the black antenna may be evident. A generalized wing shape also can be seen.

A day or two before the butterfly emerges, the chrysalis looks darker, and the orange, black, and white wing pattern is visible through the chrysalis. The drawings in Figure 8-1 show two views of a chrysalis.

Materials

For each student
   1 **Activity Sheet 7, Observing the Chrysalis**

For the class
   Butterfly flight cages
   Illustration of the chrysalis from pg. 120 to be used as an overhead
     transparency or as a bulletin board display
   Class Calendar

Figure 8-1

Two views of the chrysalis

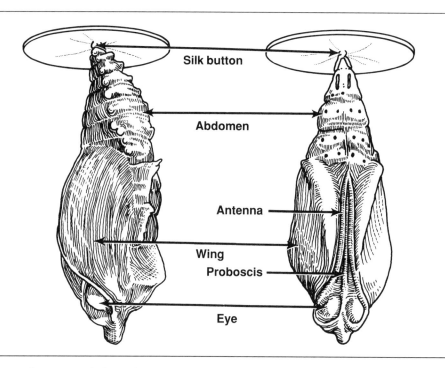

Preparation

1. Duplicate **Activity Sheet 7**.

2. Obtain and set up an overhead projector, if necessary.

Procedure

1. Review with the children what they observed when the chrysalises formed. This discussion may be easier if some of the caterpillars are still in the J-shape.

2. Cluster the children in small groups around the butterfly cages and give them time to observe the chrysalises. Remind them that the tail end of the chrysalis is attached to the silk button, and the pupa is hanging head down. Leading questions may help focus the observations:

    ■ Are there any shapes that look like they are part of a head? (eyes, antennae, proboscis)

    ■ Can students see other body parts forming? (wings, abdomen)

    ■ Can students describe the colors of the chrysalis? Ask them to be alert for any color changes that occur during the coming week. (The chrysalis will get darker shortly before emergence.)

3. Use the illustration on pg. 120 to focus attention on the developing parts. You may either use it as an overhead projection or hang it on a bulletin board.

4. Distribute either **Activity Sheet 7** or the Student Notebooks. Give students time to draw and label the chrysalis.

Final Activities

1. Add today's important observations to the **Class Calendar**.

If the chrysalises have changed color or the wings are visible, you may want to situate the flight cages in prominent places in the classroom so that students can spot the first emergence. Conduct informal observations each day until the butterflies come out.

Extensions

1. Observations of the chrysalis may be brief. You might have some time to discuss other life cycles. An oak tree is a good example. It has the following life cycle: Acorn to seedling to sapling to mature tree to dead snag to fallen tree that nourishes the soil where a new seedling sprouts. Discussion of other life cycles allows you to reinforce the idea of life cycles. It also introduces the concept of death as a necessary and natural part of all life cycles. With this knowledge, children may be able to deal more easily with any tragedies that may befall their butterflies.

2. Have students pretend that they are "the mysterious chrysalis." What is happening inside? How does it feel to experience these changes? How long will it take to change? What will it be like to emerge?

3. Puppets are a fun way to dramatize the life cycle of a Painted Lady. You may want to make several sets of puppets as a class project, or enlist the help of a parent to make a set for you. Decorate a long sock to simulate a caterpillar. Find a paper bag to be the chrysalis and decorate it, too. Create a clothespin butterfly with four paper wings, two pipe cleaner antennae, and six legs. Figure 8-2 shows some examples of these puppets.

Figure 8-2

Puppets showing the life cycle of the Painted Lady butterfly

A. The caterpillar "bunched up"   **B. Caterpillar grows larger**

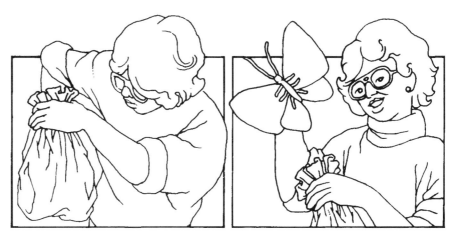

C. The caterpillar becomes a chrysalis   **D. The chrysalis becomes a butterfly**

Now use your puppets to dramatize the life of a Painted Lady.

■ Begin with the caterpillar sock puppet scrunched up some, so that as you or the children tell the story the caterpillar can grow larger and larger.

■ You may want to have some thread on hand as a prop so that the caterpillar can spin silk and later make a button to hang from.

■ When you come to the part of the story where the caterpillar transforms into a chrysalis, place your whole hand into the paper bag, as shown in Figure 8-2. Remove the caterpillar puppet while your hand is hidden in the chrysalis and pick up the butterfly puppet, which you have hidden in the bag earlier.

■ Emerge with a flourish as a butterfly.

Observing the Chrysalis **Activity Sheet 7**

Name: _____

Date: _____

Use your hand lens to observe a chrysalis. Draw what you see.

Did you see these parts? Check them off if you did.

____ Eye

____ Antenna

____ Proboscis

____ Wing

____ Abdomen

LESSON 9	# The Butterfly Emerges

Overview

An exciting event heralds the opening of this lesson. After 7 to 10 days in the chrysalis, the butterflies finally emerge. First, they "pump up" their wings and hang them out to dry and harden. Then they are ready for flight.

Objectives

■ Students observe the butterflies emerging from the chrysalis (or discover the butterfly and empty chrysalis case).

■ Students observe some distinct butterfly body parts.

Background

There have been signs that the butterfly is about to emerge: each chrysalis has darkened, and the orange and black wing patterns have become visible through the chrysalis. When it finally happens, the emergence takes only about 30 seconds. First, a small crack appears along the back of the chrysalis, followed by another crack along the side; these openings free the butterfly's back and six legs. Finally, the butterfly steps out of its chrysalis, pulling its wings and abdomen clear of its case.

When the butterfly first emerges, the wings are small and soft and slightly crumpled. The butterfly positions itself so that the wings hang downward. It then contracts its body, which forces fluids into the wings and makes them expand. In about 2 to 3 hours, the wings will be fully expanded and hardened and ready to fly. The drawings in Figure 9-1 show the butterfly emerging and expanding its wings.

While the wings are hardening, the butterfly begins the important task of joining the two sections of its proboscis—the coiled, straw-like tongue used to siphon nectar from flowers. While the proboscis is still soft and pliable, the butterfly rhythmically works the two halves from side to side as a way to connect the interlocking spines. Once a connection has been made at the head, the butterfly quickly zips together the remainder of the spines, down to the tiny delicate tip. For the first day or two after emerging, the butterflies do not require food and probably won't accept any. (See Lesson 10 for complete information on feeding.)

Figure 9-1

The butterfly emerges

A. The butterfly when
it first emerges

B. Several hours
later, after the wings
have expanded and
hardened

You will notice a red liquid coming from the tail end of the butterfly. This is **meconium**, or waste tissue, that is left over from metamorphosis. Assure your class that this is not blood; the butterflies simply are getting rid of some waste.

Once in a while, a butterfly emerges with deformed wings that will not expand and straighten out. This is unfortunate, but it is also one of those teachable moments. If questions arise, take the opportunity to discuss the butterfly's deformity and perhaps to relate it to human disabilities.

If a butterfly escapes, be assured that you can pick it up without doing too much damage to it. Try to avoid capturing a butterfly in a small container or in cupped hands. Instead, gently pinch the front edge of the butterfly's wings together over its back. If you wait until the butterfly has alighted, sometimes you can get it to walk onto your finger.

Materials

For each student

1 **Activity Sheet 8, The Life Cycle of a Butterfly**

For the class

Butterfly flight cages
Class Calendar
Art materials

Preparation

1. Duplicate **Activity Sheet 8**.

2. Obtain any art supplies you may need.

3. If you decide to have the students make a life cycle wheel as described in No. 6 of the Procedures section below, duplicate one set of the black line masters on pgs. 61, 62, and 63 for each student. (This optional activity is not in the Student Notebook.)

Procedure

1. Enjoy the wonder of this miraculous transformation along with your class! There will be considerable excitement when the first butterfly is discovered, and all the children will rush to see it. Because of the high level of excitement, the children probably will be unable to make any careful observations right now, but listen for any comments they make or the mention of any body parts. This will tell you the vocabulary they already know and pave the way for a more formal study of butterfly parts in Lesson 11.

2. Next, ask if anyone observed where the butterfly came from. The empty chrysalis case is quite noticeable. Often the newly emerged butterfly will be hanging from the case or will be nearby. Later, remove the empty chrysalis from the box for the children to see. Have them observe how it is split from end to end.

3. As butterflies emerge over the next several days, encourage your students to continue making frequent observations. Specifically, ask them to look for:

   ■ newly emerged butterflies pumping up their wings

   ■ butterflies in the process of joining the two halves of the proboscis

   ■ empty chrysalises

   ■ differences in coloration between the tops of the wings and their undersides

   ■ how the butterfly uses its feet, wings, antennae, and proboscis

   This also will help prepare them for the closer observations of butterfly body parts and their functions that will be discussed in Lesson 11.

4. Pass out copies of **Activity Sheet 8, The Life Cycle of a Butterfly**, and let students conduct a sequencing activity with the pictures of the butterfly in various stages of its life cycle.

5. Students also can use **Activity Sheet 8** to make headbands or necklaces that they can wear home to explain the life cycle of the butterfly to their families. Or, save the headbands for your class to wear during the release of the butterflies ceremony in Lesson 12.

   Below are the directions for making these ornaments.

   ■ To make a headband, glue the pictures from **Activity Sheet 8** to a long (3" x 20") strip of paper.

   ■ To make a necklace, punch a hole at the top of each picture and string the pictures on a piece of yarn.

6. Another way to use the pictures from **Activity Sheet 8** is in a life cycle wheel. The following illustrations and instructions will help students make the wheel.

The Butterfly Emerges / **59**

Instructions for making the Life Cycle Wheel:

1. Cut out Section A, the life cycle wheel, from pg. 61. Cut out the life cycle pictures from pg. 62.

2. Paste the life cycle pictures in the correct sequence to the life cycle wheel.

3. Cut out Section B, the cover wheel, from pg. 63. Then cut out the window on the cover wheel.

4. Assemble the two wheels by pushing a brass fastener through the dot marked in the center of each wheel (Figure 9-2).

5. Rotate the handles. You should see each stage of the butterfly's life cycle through the window on the cover wheel.

Figure 9-2

How to make a life cycle wheel

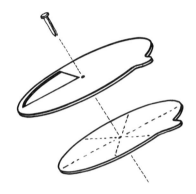 

Final Activities

1. Hold a brief class discussion about what students observed today.

2. Record the important observations on the **Class Calendar**. Draw a box around this date. You will need this information again in Lesson 13.

Extensions

Some classes have enjoyed handing out butterfly-shaped crackers as "emergence announcements" to the principal, other teachers, or other classes in the school.

Evaluation

The life cycle headband may be used to evaluate a student's ability to sequentially order the life stages of the butterfly. If you choose to help students make the life cycle wheel, it too may be used for this purpose.

Section A
Life cycle wheel

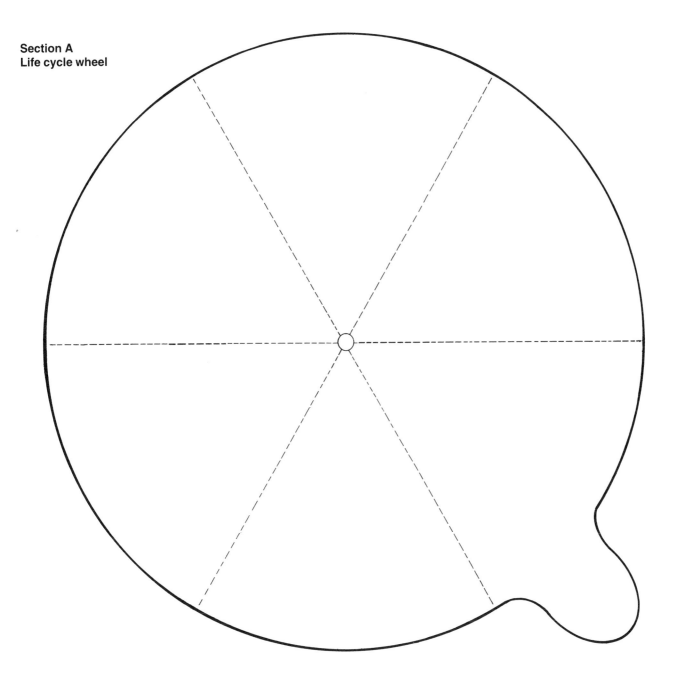

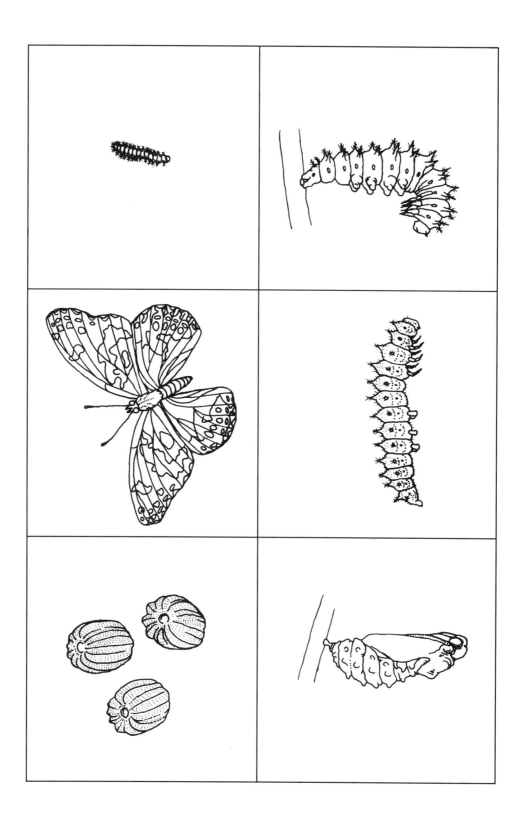

**Section B
Cover wheel
and window**

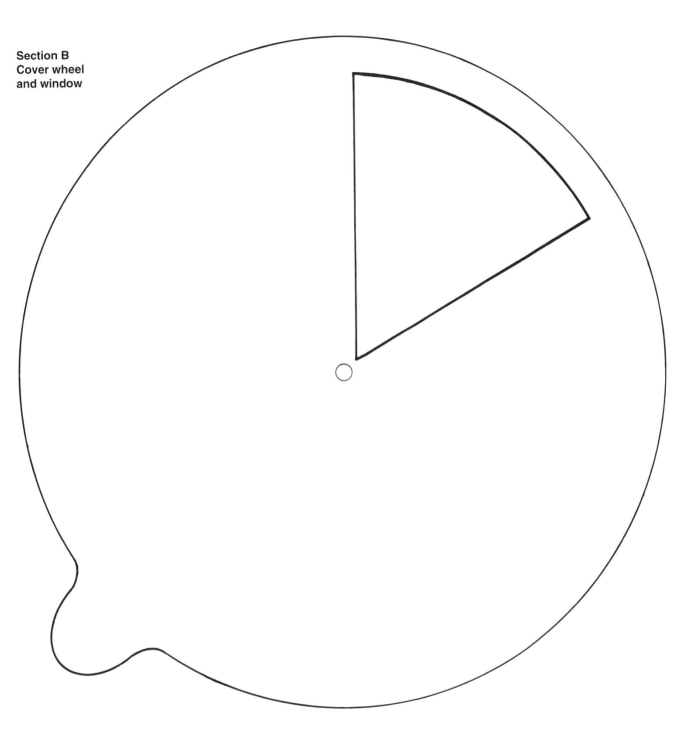

The Life Cycle of a Butterfly

Activity Sheet 8

Name: _

Write the date the butterflies emerged:

1. Color the pictures of the butterfly's life on the second page.

2. Cut out the pictures you colored.

3. Paste the pictures in the correct order below to show the butterfly's life.

Activity Sheet 8

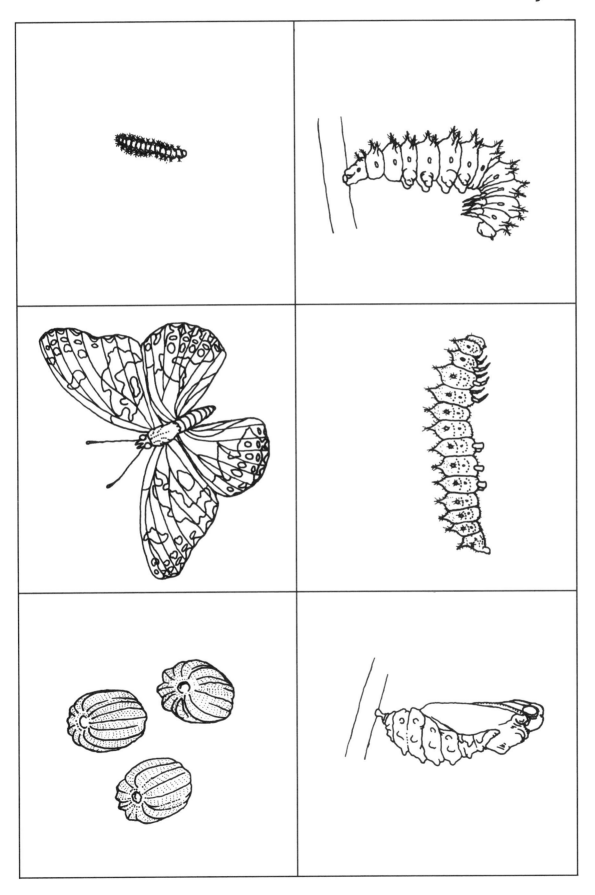

Feeding the Butterflies

Overview

A day or two after emerging, the butterflies will need food. The children will find it satisfying to answer this need. They also will have ample opportunity to observe the butterfly's specialized proboscis in action.

Objectives

- Students compare the way a butterfly eats with the way a caterpillar eats.
- Students observe how the butterfly uses the proboscis to eat.

Background

Different types of insects have different types of mouths. Insect mouth parts are highly specialized structures that determine what food the insect can eat. In the course of metamorphosis, the mouth parts of the Painted Lady changed from the chewing mandibles of the caterpillar stage to the sucking proboscis of the butterfly. While a caterpillar can chew only leafy food with its laterally moving jaws, the butterfly can suck only liquid food through its tube-like proboscis.

A butterfly carries its long proboscis coiled up close to its head, as shown in Figure 10-1. It is nearly as long as the butterfly's body and is easily seen. In nature, this long tube serves the butterfly well, allowing it to reach deep down into a flower to sip nectar.

In Step 1 of the **Preparation** section, there is a recipe for a sugar-water feeding solution and instructions on how to set up a feeding station. The food supply needs to be replenished every day, so keep the sugar water recipe handy. The children also might want to bring in natural foods for the butterflies; suggestions are given in Step 3 of the **Preparation** section. Natural foods allow you to underscore once again the idea that these butterflies are wild creatures and that they will be returning to nature.

Materials

For each student

1 **Activity Sheet 9, Butterflies Need Food**

Figure 10-1

The butterfly's head

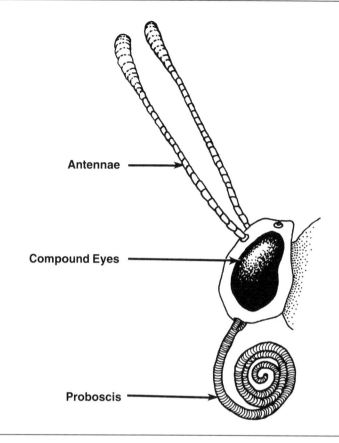

Antennae

Compound Eyes

Proboscis

For the class

> 4   feeding stations (2 for each cage) consisting of:
>
> > Sugar
> > Water
> > Sponge pieces
> > Petri dishes or shallow jar lids
>
> Paper cups
>
> 1   spoon
> **Class Calendar**

Preparation

1.   To make a feeding solution for the adult Painted Lady, **mix together 1 teaspoon of sugar and 1/2 cup of water** in the paper cup. Cut the two sponges into four equal pieces. Saturate a piece of sponge with the sugar-water solution. Place the sponge in a petri dish or a shallow jar lid. Put the setup on the floor of the butterfly cage.

2.   Be sure to replenish the food supply at least once a day.

3.   The butterflies will accept a wide variety of natural foods, as shown below. You might try a solution of 1 part water to 1 part honey, a small chunk of fresh melon, or an apple. Fresh flowers of almost any kind will work, too. They should be placed in a **narrow-necked** bottle of water so the butterflies won't drown (Figure 10-2). Some of the Painted Lady's favorite flowers are thistle, rose of Sharon, hollyhock, marsh mallow, and buddleia.

Figure 10-2

*Food for
the butterflies*

Fresh flowers in a
narrow-necked jar

Sugar and
water solution

Honey and
water solution

Procedure

1. Ask students to name some different ways that people eat. Examples include biting, chewing, sipping, sucking, licking.

2. Review how the caterpillar ate (biting, chewing). Then ask students for their ideas on how butterflies eat (sipping, sucking, drinking). Accept all student responses for now.

3. Tell students that today they will observe the butterflies eating. Describe the sugar-water solution you have prepared. Ask students to imagine how they would "eat" the sugar water. Would it be the same way they would eat a leaf?

4. Gather the class around the butterfly cages. Place feeding stations inside each cage. Allow students time to observe what happens.

5. Ask students what the butterflies are doing. Typical responses might include:

    ■ flying or walking to the food

    ■ walking on the food (butterflies taste with their feet!)

    ■ moving the antennae (to smell), touching things with the antennae

    ■ uncoiling the proboscis

6. Ask students why they think the butterfly is uncoiling its proboscis (to eat). Ask, how can you eat through a long tube like that? (By sipping, as people do through a straw.)

Final Activities

1. Talk with the class about where they have seen butterflies feeding outside. Have they seen that butterflies suck the sweet nectar from deep inside the flowers, using their long proboscis?

2. Encourage students to bring in other foods for the butterflies to try. Caution them not to pick flowers without permission.

3. Read through **Activity Sheet 9** with the class. Give students time to complete it. Then collect the student work.

4. Record today's observations on the **Class Calendar**.

Extensions

1. Hold a Lepidopterist Lunch! (A lepidopterist is someone who studies butterflies.) You could have a leafy green salad to crunch like a caterpillar, and sweet juice to sip through a straw like a butterfly.

2. As a language arts activity, write a good-bye message or poem in preparation for the release ceremony. You also could write invitations to the ceremony to other classes, parents, or teachers.

Evaluation

Ask students to compare the way a caterpillar eats with the way a butterfly eats. They should mention these differences:

■ A caterpillar chews its food but a butterfly sips it.

■ A caterpillar eats leaves (solid) but a butterfly drinks nectar (liquid).

Butterflies Need Food   **Activity Sheet 9**

Name: _____

Date: _____

The butterflies will want to eat.
They will stand on the sponge and drink the sugar water.
The sponge will get dry.
Add more sugar water to the sponge every day.

What will the butterflies eat outside?

_____

_____

_____

The butterfly has a long tube for a mouth.
The tube is called a proboscis.
Draw the proboscis on this butterfly.

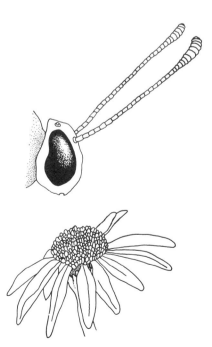

The Butterfly's Body

Overview

After the excitement of watching the butterflies emerge from the chrysalises and take their first nourishment, students are ready to make closer observations of the butterfly body parts. They will relate the butterfly parts to their own body parts and compare their relative functions.

Objectives

■ Students observe the physical characteristics and the behavior of their butterflies.

■ Students compare the butterflies to themselves.

■ The teacher further prepares students for the release of the butterflies by helping them see how butterflies are equipped to survive in the natural world.

Background

The butterfly's body is quite complex and very well adapted for survival. Like all insects, its body is divided into three main parts: the head, the thorax (or midsection), and the abdomen. Below is a discussion of these three parts and their functions.

The head has a pair of sensitive antennae that are used for both touch and smell. A pair of compound eyes that are large and rounded see color well. Together, the eyes and the antennae give the butterfly the ability to find food, to recognize a potential mate, and to select the appropriate plant material on which to lay its eggs. The long sucking mouth tube, the proboscis, remains coiled when not in use. Uncoiled, it is nearly as long as the adult's body and can reach into the deep recesses of a flower to drink nectar.

The thorax, or midsection, holds both the two pairs of wings and the three pairs of jointed legs. Besides providing mobility, the Painted Lady's wings display a distinctive pattern that can be recognized by others of its kind. Wings also protect the butterfly in two ways: by giving it a way to escape from predators and by camouflaging it. The two sides of the wings have different colors and different patterns. While the underside is a muted combination of white, brown, tan, black, blue, and purple, the top side is a more vivid combination of white, orange, black, and brown.

The butterfly, like all insects, has six jointed legs, but because the Painted Lady's first pair of legs is very small, only four are easily visible. Surprisingly, the butterfly tastes with its second and third pairs of feet.

The abdomen is the last body section. In females, it is somewhat more rounded. At the tip of this section are the sexual organs. You may see pairs of butterflies copulating, joined end to end. Figure 11-1 shows two views of a butterfly. In both pictures, the parts have been labeled.

Figure 11-1

*Two views of a
butterfly's body*

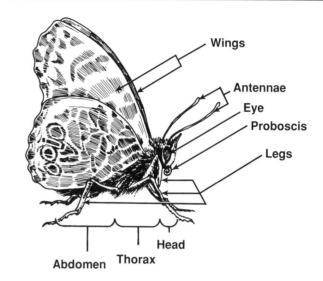

A. Side view

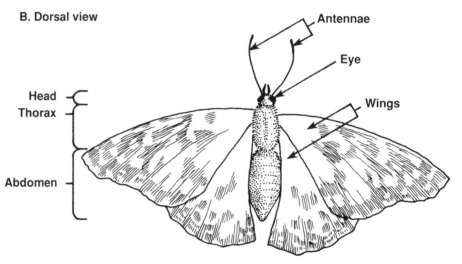

B. Dorsal view

Materials

For each student

  1 **Activity Sheet 10, My Butterfly and Me**

For the class

  Butterfly flight cages

  Class Calendar

  Overhead projector or bulletin board display

Preparation

1. Duplicate **Activity Sheet 10.**

2. Display the illustrations of the two views of the butterfly on pg. 121 either on the bulletin board or as an overhead transparency.

Procedure

1. Allow students sufficient time to observe the adult Painted Ladies before conducting this lesson. During the observation periods, direct student attention to the butterfly body parts and how they are used.

2. Hold a class discussion about what students have observed about butterfly body parts and how they are used. You may want to use the illustrations on pg. 121 either as a bulletin board display or as an overhead projection to help focus the discussion. Try to listen for some of the words students have used when they were making informal observations. The following questions may help children identify the parts and recognize how they are useful to the butterfly in the real world:

    ■ Look at the butterfly's head. What other body parts do you find on the head? (Eyes, antennae, and proboscis.)

    ■ What do you think the butterfly uses these parts for? (Eyes: to see color well, to find food, to find a mate. Antennae: for touch and smell. Proboscis: to reach nectar deep inside the flowers.)

    ■ Count the wings. How many are there? (Four.)

    ■ What does a butterfly use its wings for? (To fly to food and to the plants that it lays its eggs on; to fly away from predators; for camouflage.)

    ■ How many legs are there? (Six, but only four are clearly visible.)

    ■ What does a butterfly use its legs for? (To walk and to taste.)

    ■ Have you noticed any butterflies mating? What parts of their bodies were joined? (The ends of the abdomens.)

3. Distribute **Activity Sheet 10** (or the student booklets, if you are using them). Preview the activity sheet with the class. Allow students sufficient time to complete the sheet.

Final Activities

1. As a follow-up to the activity sheet, ask students to compare their bodies and the butterflies' bodies. How are the two alike? How are they different?

2. Record today's important observations on the **Class Calendar**.

Extensions

1. If a butterfly dies, gently remove it from the cage and have children look at it closely with a hand lens.

2. As an art project, ask children to illustrate the different ways a butterfly uses its wings: to fly to food, to find a mate, to escape enemies, for camouflage.

3. Make butterfly kites. See the directions on the pg. 76.

The next lesson is the release ceremony. You probably will find it useful to arrange for several other adults to help you manage the class outdoors.

Plan ahead for the release ceremony to make it a real celebration. You may want to invite parents, recite a farewell poem, decorate T-shirts, dramatize the life cycle, or enjoy some butterfly cookies. See the **Extensions** section in Lesson 12 for additional suggestions.

Figure 11-2

*Directions for
making a
butterfly kite*

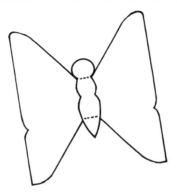

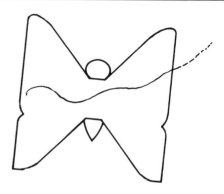

Have students cut out the two patterns on pg. 77 and paint or color them. Glue or staple the body to the center of the kite.

Place a 2-foot piece of string across the middle of the kite. One end of the string should extend to the edge of the wing.

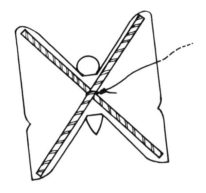

Glue or tape two straws onto the kite to form an X on top of the string. Tie the string around the straws.

Then hold the string and run with the kite. It will flutter behind you like a butterfly.

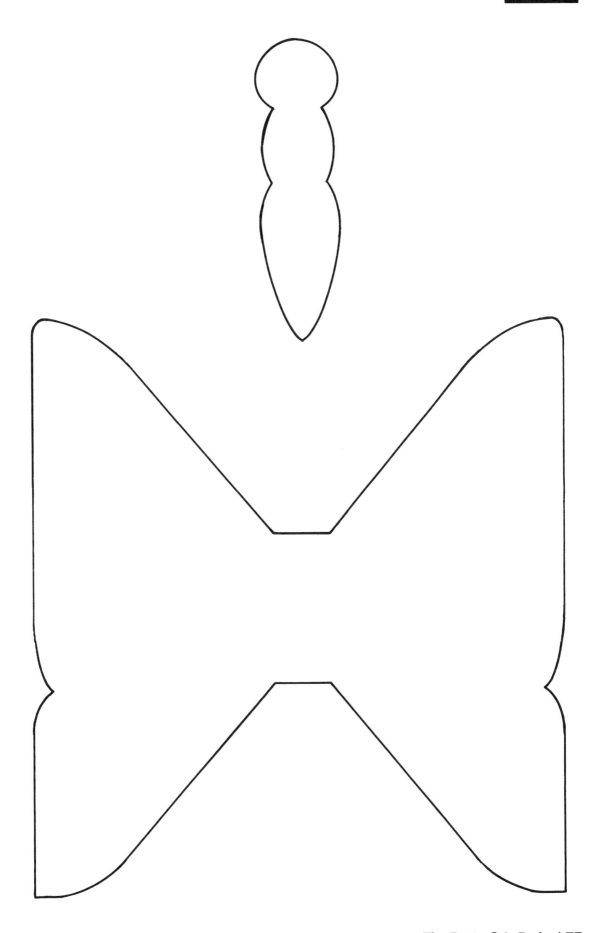

The Butterfly's Body / **77**

My Butterfly and Me   **Activity Sheet 10**

Name: _____
          _____

Date: _____
          _____

Answer these questions:

I have how many?   My butterfly has how many?
___ Legs   ___ Legs
___ Eyes   ___ Eyes
___ Wings   ___ Wings
___ Arms   ___ Arms
___ Antennae   ___ Antennae

What does a butterfly use its wings for?

_____
_____
_____
_____

What parts of its body does a butterfly use to find food?

_____
_____
_____
_____

Think about this:
    How is your butterfly like you? How is it different?

The Butterflies Go Free

Overview

In this lesson, the children release the butterflies. They come to understand that as wild creatures, the butterflies are part of the natural world and belong out in it.

Objectives

■   Students realize that butterflies have their place in the environment.

Background

In many ways, you have been preparing your students for this day ever since the caterpillars first arrived. Although it may be difficult for the children to say good-bye to the butterflies, the butterflies are better off in their natural environment, where they have room to fly, can find a variety of foods, and can mate and then lay eggs to produce the next generation. Butterflies also are beneficial to their environment. Not only are they beautiful, but they pollinate flowers and provide food for birds and other animals.

An adult Painted Lady butterfly only lives for about two weeks even under the best of conditions, so you will want to select a time for the release that takes this into account. Allow about 5 to 7 days for student observation, then let the butterflies go. If they are indoors much longer, the possibility of tattered wings, injuries, and even death becomes more likely. If one of the butterflies dies, the children may become upset. You will want to recognize and be sensitive to these feelings. You also may want to use this opportunity to discuss death as a natural part of the life cycle. There are some excellent trade books on the subject. See the **Bibliography, Appendix E.**

Plan to release the butterflies when the outside temperature has reached 60°F (15°C) or higher. In planning where the release should take place, survey your schoolyard for possibilities. Ideally, the location should provide leaves for a resting place and cover and flowers for a food source. Butterflies compete very well in the natural environment, and often are seen in the vicinity for several days after their release.

Materials

For each student
  1   headband or necklace made in Lesson 9 (optional)
      Writing paper

For the class
>   Butterfly flight cages
>   **Class Calendar**

Preparation

1. Select a date and time of day for the release of the butterflies.

2. Take the class outside to survey the schoolyard and select a site for the release.

3. Consider inviting guests to the release ceremony. Send invitations to other classes, parents, or the principal.

4. Recruit several other adults to help.

5. Read the **Extensions** section in this lesson and obtain materials for any of the projects you plan to do.

Procedure

1. Before releasing the butterflies, hold a brief discussion indoors about it. Ask the class, "Do you think we should keep the butterflies in the box or let them go? Try to give a reason for your answer." Typically, students will respond that they want to keep the butterflies because they are pretty and interesting to watch. Some also may express concern that the butterflies will not be able to fend for themselves.

    But most students will recognize that the butterflies can survive in the outside world because that is their natural home. The advantages of letting them go are that they will have more space, they will be able to find flowers, and they will mate and produce eggs, thus ensuring that there will be more butterflies.

2. Take the cages outside and have students sit around them. This might be a good time to recite a butterfly poem. See the **Bibliography** on pg. 109 for suggestions. Reciting poems or telling stories written by the students or singing a song would also be appropriate.

3. Open the cages and wait patiently. It will take some time for the butterflies to find their way out of the cages and fly off. Ask children to notice where they land and how their coloring helps camouflage them. Observe, too, how they fly. Is it in a straight line, up and down, or zigzag?

4. After a final farewell, return to the classroom to talk and write about the experience.

Final Activities

1. Ask children to imagine how different their butterfly's life is now that it is free. Either record their thoughts for them or ask them to write their ideas. Students can write their thoughts in the appropriate place in their student booklets or on writing paper.

2. Record today's release ceremony on the **Class Calendar**.

3. Inspect the butterfly cages for eggs. Look especially at the paper towels used to line the cages and at any leaves or flowers. The eggs are a blue-green color and very tiny. Use a magnifying glass to help you find them.

    If you are lucky enough to find eggs, you are now faced with the challenge of what to do with them. The simplest solution is to place them outside on one of their preferred food plants. A more complicated but very exciting option is to raise a second generation. See **Appendix D** for complete instructions.

Extensions

1. View the filmstrip, "Painted Lady Butterfly," from Insect Lore Products. (Call 1-800-LIVE-BUG for more information.) It is an excellent review of the entire life of this butterfly, and helps place it in its natural outdoor setting.

2. Food always makes the release memorable for children. Consider providing some butterfly crackers and decorated cookies or cupcakes as a special treat.

3. Use fabric crayons (available in craft shops) on clean cotton T-shirts to create wearable souvenirs of the project. Children could draw the life cycle or their favorite part of it on the shirts.

Using Our Data

Overview

In this lesson, students review the unit by revisiting all the work they have produced. After reviewing the materials, students use their own data to answer their questions about the life cycle of the butterfly.

Objectives

■ Students use their data to answer their questions.

Background

Students will be pleasantly surprised by the amount of information they have recorded about caterpillars and butterflies and by how much more they know about the life cycle of butterflies. It is a satisfying experience for students to take stock and measure their own progress. By working with **Activity Sheet 11**, students will be able to discover for themselves how long it takes for a caterpillar to become a butterfly.

Materials

For each student

> All of their written products from the unit (except for the drawings they did of what they thought a butterfly looked like—done in Lesson 7)

1 **Activity Sheet 11, From Caterpillar to Butterfly**

For the class

> **Class Calendar**

Preparation

1. Duplicate **Activity Sheet 11**.

Procedure

1. Give students their work from this lesson or their Student Notebooks. Allow time for students to review their work.

2. Ask students to pay special attention to the different stages of the butterfly's life cycle they have recorded. Listen to their informal remarks for spontaneous use of vocabulary terms related to butterfly body parts and behavior.

3. Congratulate students on their fine collection of data about butterflies. Tell them that they have been working the way scientists work—observing and making records of their observations over a long period of time. Note that after scientists have collected a lot of information, they use it to answer questions. Indicate to the class that now they are going to use the class collection of information to answer some questions about the life of the butterfly.

4. Distribute **Activity Sheet 11, From Caterpillar to Butterfly**. Ask students to find the dates in their own data or on the **Class Calendar** and to record them in the first section. (These dates are the dates on **Activity Sheets 1, 6, and 8** from Lessons 2, 7, and 9.)

5. In the second section of the **Activity Sheet**, ask students to compare the duration of the caterpillar stage (usually 7 to 10 days) with the duration of the chrysalis stage (usually 12 to 18 days). Then have students add up the two numbers to get the total time of transition from caterpillar to butterfly.

6. The last two questions on the **Activity Sheet** ask students to use their data to draw conclusions about which stage was the longest and which the shortest—a very scientific exercise indeed!

Final Activities

As a summation, you might like to have students work more with the **Class Calendar**. Here are some suggestions:

■ Find the dates of important changes in the life cycle.

■ Count up the number of days each stage lasted.

■ Count up the total number of days the creatures were in the classroom.

■ Predict when the butterflies will lay eggs. (Sporadically, from about 4 days after emergence from the chrysalis on.)

■ Predict when the new eggs will hatch into caterpillars. (About 3 to 5 days after being laid.)

Extensions

1. If children have not been using *The Life Cycle of Butterflies* Student Notebooks, they might enjoy assembling their work into booklets. Here are a few ideas.

To fasten the products together:

■ staple them

■ punch holes and then insert brass fasteners

■ sew up the side with a tapestry needle and yarn

To make a cover:

■ use the butterfly life cycle as the illustration

■ ask students to create original butterfly artwork

2. Display the student work, then after you've evaluated it, let students take it home to share with their families.

From Caterpillar to Butterfly   **Activity Sheet 11**

Name: _____

Date: _____

Write the dates:

   When did the caterpillar
   come?   _____

   When did the caterpillar
   change into a chrysalis?   _____

   When did the chrysalis
   change into a butterfly?   _____

How many days did it take for:

   The caterpillar to change into a chrysalis?   [ ]

   The chrysalis to change into a butterfly?   **+** [ ]

   The caterpillar to change into a butterfly?   [ ]

   Which stage was
   the longest?   _____

   Which stage was
   the shortest?   _____

Discovering that Butterflies Are Insects

Overview

After having studied one insect closely, students now learn the characteristics all insects have in common. They apply what they have learned to distinguish an insect from a non-insect.

Objectives

■ Students learn that the butterfly is an animal called an insect.

■ Students discover the characteristics that all insects share.

Background

Nine out of every ten animals living on earth are insects. They are an immensely successful and varied group, inhabiting every environment found on earth. There are over one million different kinds of known insects, but they all share certain characteristics. Dragonflies, grasshoppers, roaches, ladybugs, bees, and butterflies are all classified as insects because they have the following characteristics:

■ six jointed legs

■ three main body parts (head, thorax, and abdomen)

■ two antennae

■ one or two pairs of wings (when they have wings)

A number of closely related animals are often confused with insects: ticks, spiders, millipedes, centipedes, and pill bugs, to name a few. But upon inspection, you will find that each fails to meet the test for insects in one way or another.

Note: On the **Activity Sheet** for this lesson, students will be asked to decide whether a spider is an insect. Try not to give the answer away during discussion.

Materials

For each student

1 **Activity Sheet 12, Are Butterflies Insects?**

For the teacher

Butterfly illustrations (pgs. 121 and 122, **Appendix F**)
Overhead projector or bulletin board display

Preparation

1. Duplicate **Activity Sheet 12**.

2. Display the butterfly illustration on pg. 121, **Appendix F** either as an overhead projection or on the bulletin board.

3. Plan to display the illustration of the butterfly and the spider on pg. 122 while the students are working with **Activity Sheet 12** toward the end of the lesson.

Figure 14-1

Side and dorsal views of a butterfly

A. Side view

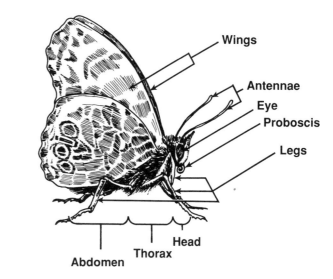

B. Dorsal view

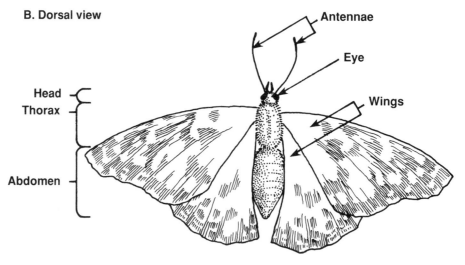

Procedure

1. Review with the class what they already know about butterfly anatomy. Use the butterfly illustration on the bulletin board or on the overhead projector to help focus attention on the body parts.

2. Introduce the idea that the butterfly belongs to a very large group of animals called insects. All insects have certain distinct body parts. Point out these body parts: six legs, three main body sections, two antennae, and two pairs of wings. (Wings are the only feature that can vary. Some insects have only one pair, and some have none.) Any animal that has all of these parts in the correct numbers can be called an insect.

3. Ask students to name some creatures they think are insects. You may want to list these on the board. If controversy arises, or you are just not

sure, use the opportunity to do some library research to check. A field guide to insects is one useful way to make accurate identifications. (See the **Bibliography** for specific resources.)

4. Distribute **Activity Sheet 12** and preview it with the class. Give students time to complete it.

Final Activities   Ask students to explain why a spider cannot be called an insect. Ask if they can think of any other creatures that might be mistaken for insects.

Extensions

1. Take a short field trip on the playground to look for other insects.

2. Ask if anyone has an insect collection they might like to share with the class.

3. As an art project, challenge students to draw a picture of an insect nobody has ever seen. It should fulfill all the requirements for an insect, but after that anything goes. They might also name their insect and discuss where it lives, what it eats, and how it protects itself.

Are Butterflies Insects?   **Activity Sheet 12**

Name: _____

_____

_____

Date: _____

_____

Look at this drawing of a butterfly.

Count how many a butterfly has:

____ Legs
____ Antennae
____ Wings
____ Main body sections

Wings

Antennae

Eye

Proboscis

Legs

Head

Thorax

Abdomen

Is the butterfly an insect?
_____

_ _

_____

Look at this drawing of a spider.

Count how many a spider has:

____ Legs
____ Antennae
____ Wings
____ Main body sections

Palp

Legs

Head and
Thorax

Abdomen

Is the spider an insect?
_____

_ _

_____

LESSON 15   Other Life Cycles

Overview

Over the course of the unit, students have become very familiar with the life cycle of one special animal. Now they will apply the life cycle concept to other plants and animals within their experience. Because of the incredible diversity of life forms, there is the potential for several rich discussions of different life cycles.

Objectives

- Students apply a concept they have learned in this unit to new situations.

- Students expand their knowledge of the life cycles of other plants and animals.

- Students realize that cycles are regenerative: life begets life.

Background

The cycle is an important concept in science. Every kind of living thing goes through a life cycle that is reliable and predictable, as well as unique to its own kind. For example, all plants have a life cycle, but flowering plants, specifically, go from seed to seedling to flower to fertilization and production of a new generation of seeds. The illustration on pg. 92 shows the life cycle of the *Brassica* plant.

Similarly, all animals have a life cycle, but the stages in the life cycle of a butterfly are quite different from the stages in the life cycle of a human being.

Our world contains an incredible diversity of life. Don't let that intimidate you or limit your class discussions. Acknowledge the differences, then let the discussion take whatever direction it will, depending on the experiences of the children in your class. The overriding idea here is to take advantage of the life cycle of the butterfly to open the students' eyes to the fact that life cycles are common to all living things, yet not all life cycles are the same. And if you find yourself not knowing about the life cycle of a particular life form under discussion, encourage the children to think about how you can find out together.

Figure 15-1

Life cycle of the Brassica *plant*

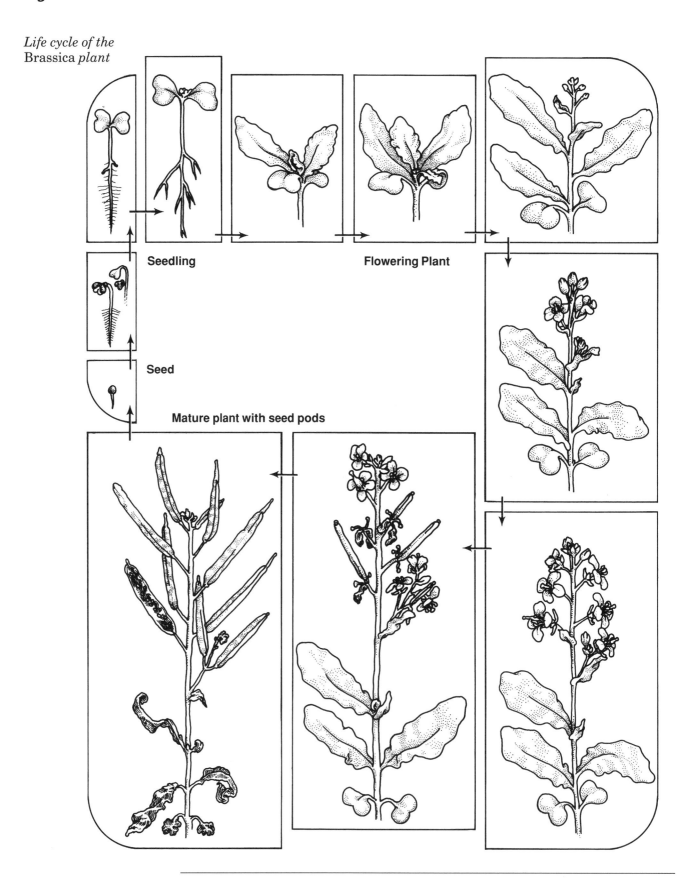

Seedling

Flowering Plant

Seed

Mature plant with seed pods

Discussion of the life cycles of other creatures might be an excellent opportunity to use the "think-pair-share" technique. For example, for Step 3 in the **Procedure** section, you could present the class with one of the questions, then ask them to go through the following three steps:

■ Think about the problem by yourself for 2 minutes.

■ Now, discuss the problem with a partner for 2 minutes.

■ Finally, share with the class what you and your partner think.

Preparation

1. Locate trade books illustrating life cycles of other creatures. (See the "Other Life Cycles" section in the **Bibliography** for suggestions.)

2. Locate pictures or posters of living creatures to use as conversation starters.

Procedure

1. Create the atmosphere for the discussion of other life cycles by displaying trade books, pictures, or posters of a variety of living creatures. Try to include as many different types of living things as possible. A representative sampling might include illustrations of some of the following:

■ a plant

■ an insect other than the butterfly

■ a fish (an egg layer or a live bearer)

■ an amphibian (such as a frog, toad, or newt)

■ a reptile (such as a turtle, snake, lizard, alligator, or dinosaur)

■ a bird

■ a mammal (don't forget humans)

2. Open the discussion by saying that now that students are very familiar with the life cycle of one insect, it might be interesting to talk about the life cycles of other life forms.

One way to get the conversational ball rolling is to ask, "Do people have a life cycle? Tell me about your life." Use leading questions to guide the discussion both forward and backward in time, such as:

■ How old are you now? How has your body changed from when you were born? How are you the same as when you were born?

■ Look into the future. How many years until you are a teenager? How will you be different then?

■ What stage of life comes next? Will you change again?

Sum up by saying that human bodies go through many changes from baby to adult and that each stage has some similarities to the others and some differences. (See Figure 15-2.)

3. Now turn the discussion to the life cycles of other creatures that your class is familiar with.

Note: Mammals have the least interesting life cycles of all creatures; we may adore babies, puppies, and bear cubs, but insect metamorphosis is much more dramatic.

Figure 15-2

Life cycle of humans

Questions that may challenge your students include the following:

- How many creatures can you think of that start their life as an egg? (Birds, most fish, insects, frogs, and reptiles are in this category.) Discuss the life cycle of one of them.

- What creatures can you think of that are born alive? (Mammals, marsupials [such as opossums and kangaroos], some snakes, some fish, and some insects are live bearers.) Discuss the life cycle of one of them.

- What is an example of a plant's life cycle? Discuss the life cycle of a fruit tree (or a tomato, bean, or pea plant).

Final Activities

Ask students to draw and label the life cycle of the creature of their choice. Have them list what that creature needs to live. To help students organize their ideas, refer back to earlier discussions about what caterpillars need.

Extensions

1. Ask students to bring in pictures of people at different stages in their lives. Arrange these sequentially on a bulletin board to illustrate a life cycle. The differences between male and female could be emphasized.

2. Play "Twenty Questions," life-cycle style. The person who will be questioned begins by giving one clue about the creature, such as, "I am thinking of a creature that ... starts life in the water (or is born with its eyes closed, or has to be fed by its mother when it is a baby, or lives in a nest for part of its life, or is a larva for part of its life)." Then the rest of the class asks questions to discover what the creature is.

3. Read a trade book about a life cycle. Many excellent selections are referenced in the **Bibliography**.

4. Take a walk outside to look for evidence of other life cycles.

Draw the life cycle of another plant or animal.

Post-Unit Assessments

Overview

- Assessment 1 is a follow-up to the student brainstorming sessions about caterpillars and butterflies.

- Assessment 2 asks students to draw a butterfly and compare it with the one they drew at the end of Lesson 7.

- Assessment 3 asks students to write about the life cycle of a butterfly from egg to egg.

Objectives

- Students evaluate their own progress.

- The teacher evaluates student progress.

ASSESSMENT 1

Following Up on the Student Brainstorming Sessions about Caterpillars and Butterflies

Materials

The student-generated lists saved from the brainstorming sessions.

Procedure

Display the lists and look at them with the students. Here are some ways to approach analyzing the lists to point out student progress:

- Ask students to point out statements on the lists that they now know to be true without a doubt. What experiences did they have during the unit that confirmed these statements? Leading questions may be helpful, such as "How do you know that?" and "Tell what happened next."

- Ask students to correct or improve statements. Have students give reasons for the corrections.

- Ask students to contribute new information to the lists. What else have they learned?

Final Activities

Applaud students for their progress!

ASSESSMENT 2   Comparison Drawing of the Butterfly

Materials

For each student

1   sheet of drawing paper

1   drawing of a butterfly done in Lesson 1
    Crayons

Preparation

1.   Prepare a display area (bulletin board or clothesline). Give the area a title, such as "Look How Much We Have Learned about Butterflies."

2.   Retrieve the students' original drawings of a butterfly from Lesson 1.

Procedure

1.   Tell the class that today they will see for themselves how much they have learned about butterflies. Remind them of their previous drawings, which you have kept safe (and hidden). Tell them that they each will compare their old drawings with today's new one. Assure them that they will be pleased to see how much they have learned.

2.   Instruct students to draw a butterfly with as many details as they can remember. Ask them to pay attention to the numbers of parts (such as legs, eyes, and wings) and to where the parts are located.

3.   When everyone is finished, pass out the old drawings and let the children compare the two to evaluate their own progress.

4.   Display the "before" and "after" pictures side by side on the bulletin board or clothesline. Give the students time to look at each other's work. Stress that this is a time to notice how much they have all learned and an opportunity to congratulate one another. The teacher might model an observation to set a positive tone.

ASSESSMENT 3   Writing about the Life of a Butterfly

Materials

For each student

   Pencils

   Paper

Procedure

1.   Ask students to imagine the eggs that their butterflies laid outside after they were released.

2.   Now, have them imagine what happens to the eggs. Tell them to write the life story of that egg. Emphasize that the story should begin and end with the egg.

Teacher's Record Chart of Student Progress for *The Life Cycle of Butterflies*

	Student																					
PRODUCTS Lesson 1: Drawings of caterpillar and its changes																						
Lesson 2: Activity Sheet 1. Caterpillar Food																						
Lesson 3: Activity Sheet 2, Taking Care of My Caterpillar																						
Lesson 4: Activity Sheet 3, Observing My Caterpillar																						
Lesson 5: Activity Sheet 4, My Caterpillar and Me																						
Lesson 6: Activity Sheet 5, A Caterpillar and Its Silk																						
Lesson 7: Activity Sheet 6, What Happens to the Caterpillar?																						
Lesson 7: Detailed drawing of a caterpillar																						
Lesson 8: Activity Sheet 7, Observing the Chrysalis																						
Lesson 9: Activity Sheet 8, The Life Cycle of a Butterfly																						
Lesson 10: Activity Sheet 9, Butterflies Need Food																						
Lesson 11: Activity Sheet 10, My Butterfly and Me																						
Lesson 13: Activity Sheet 11, From Caterpillar to Butterfly																						
Lesson 14: Activity Sheet 12, Are Butterflies Insects?																						
Lesson 15: Drawing of another life cycle																						
LEARNING GOALS Can use a magnifier effectively																						
Is aware of the needs of living things																						
Can observe growth, changes, and behaviors of the caterpillars and keep written record of observations																						
Can identify the head, two kinds of legs, eyes, mouth, and bristles																						
Has observed a caterpillar molting																						
Has observed evidence of changes in caterpillars: shed skin, head capsule, frass, silk																						
Can make reasonable predictions about stages in the life of a butterfly																						
Understands why a caterpillar molts																						
Has observed the J-shape stage and recorded observations																						
Has observed the chrysalis and recorded observations																						
Can identify the four wings, six legs, two antennae, proboscis, and eyes																						
Can compare the way a butterfly eats with the way a caterpillar eats																						
Understands that butterflies have their place in the environment																						
Can organize data and use it to answer questions																						
Can distinguish an insect from a non-insect																						
Understands that butterflies go through a life cycle and can sequence it correctly																						
GENERAL SKILLS Follows directions																						
Records observations with drawings of words																						
Works cooperatively																						
Contributes to discussions																						

A Chinese Legend and the History of Silk

**Reading
Selection**

A Chinese Legend

There are several different legends about how silk was discovered, yet they all begin the same way. Thousands of years ago, a young woman (some say a princess) was walking in a beautiful garden. There she spied a curious object stuck on a mulberry twig. It was fuzzy, white, and rounded in shape. She broke off the twig and took the strange object home.

Some legends say the young woman accidentally dropped the fuzzy object into a cup of hot tea. Others say she dropped it in her hot bath water. In any case, when the fuzzy object became soaked with hot liquid, it began to unravel. When it was completely unwound, what had been a wet lump was now a beautiful, shiny strand 3,000 feet long. The woman had discovered silk.

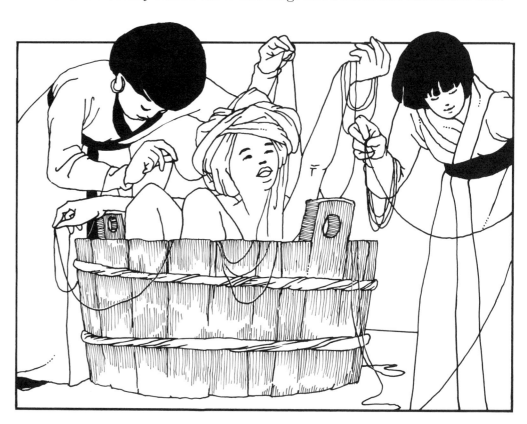

Although she didn't know it at the time, the young woman had also discovered an important insect. At the center of the tangled silk strand was a strange brown shape. According to one legend, the woman kept this strange brown shape and was surprised one day to see it turn into a hairy white moth. Today, this insect is known as the silkworm moth.

The protective covering that these moth caterpillars spin soon became an elegant garment for Chinese royalty. During the next centuries, silk became very valuable. It was used as currency, as a reward for service to the emperor, as a ceremonial garb, and as a gift to foreign rulers. People around the world marveled at the rare fabric and wondered how it was made.

The Chinese kept the source of the beautiful cloth a secret. Chinese fabric makers were threatened with death if they told how the silk was made. But, finally, the secret got out. One story says that in the 6th century B.C., monks smuggled silkworm eggs from China to Constantinople in hollow walking sticks.

The History of Silk

Silk is produced in many places today, but the countries of China, Japan, India, and Italy are most famous for their silk. At one time, people wanted to raise the caterpillars and produce silk in the United States. But there was a problem: Mulberry trees don't grow as well in the United States as they do in China, and silkworms only eat mulberry leaves—lots of them!

The first person to bring silkworms and mulberry trees to the United States was James Oglethorpe, founder of Savannah, Georgia. But, he had trouble growing enough mulberry trees to feed the caterpillars. Then, in 1869, a scientist near Boston brought some gypsy moths from Europe. He wanted to mate gypsy moths, which eat the leaves from many kinds of trees, with silkworm moths and get a silk-producing insect that would not be a picky eater. Unfortunately, the experiment became a disaster when the gypsy moths escaped from the laboratory. Hungry gypsy moth caterpillars have been gobbling up the leaves on our forest trees ever since.

Today, no silkworms live in the wild. They are domesticated and kept in cages in spotless silkworm factories. After mating, one female moth may lay 300 to 500 eggs. These eggs can be kept in a refrigerator over the winter and then brought out to hatch in the spring.

Several times each day, workers give the caterpillars fresh, tender mulberry leaves. The caterpillars grow and molt four times. When they are ready to pupate, the caterpillars spin a silk cocoon, inside which they can become pupae.

Some of the pupae are allowed to turn into moths and mate and lay eggs for the next generation. But, most of the cocoons are soaked in hot water to dissolve the sticky substance that cements the silk together. The silk unravels in a continuous thread and is wound onto spools to be spun, dyed, and woven. This all must be done before the pupa turns into a moth because, if the insect emerges from the cocoon, the strand of thread is broken into many pieces.

Many cocoons are needed to make cloth: 110 for a necktie, 630 for a blouse, and about 3,000 for a long kimono. Imagine how many worms it would take to spin the silk for a whole rack of dresses.

Notes: Some children may be upset by the fact that pupae are killed by the boiling water during the silk production process. Pictures of silkworms and the silk production process can be found in *The Silkworm Story*, a trade book listed in the **Bibliography**. Silkworm eggs or larvae also can be purchased from biological supply houses. You may raise them in your classroom using fresh mulberry leaves or a synthetically produced food.

How to Make Free or Low-Cost Butterfly Cages

If you would like to make cages, here are some suggestions of how to make some fairly easily and inexpensively. Different possibilities are shown in Figure C-1.

1. Replace the fabric on a big old lamp shade frame with dark-colored nylon netting.

2. Cut a large window in a cardboard box, leaving about a 1-inch frame around the edges. Cover the window openings with dark-colored nylon netting, taped or stapled into place.

Figure C-1

Materials for building butterfly cages

3. Punch holes in the lid of a large glass jar or plastic box.

4. For a hanging cage, try the one illustrated in Figure C-2. Materials for one cage include:
   - 1   wire coat hanger
   - 5   feet of nylon netting in a dark color
   -      Heavy cardboard or an aluminum pie plate for the floor
   -      Heavy twine
   -      Paper clips
   -      Needle and thread or toothpicks to close up the side seam

Figure C-2

A completed hanging cage

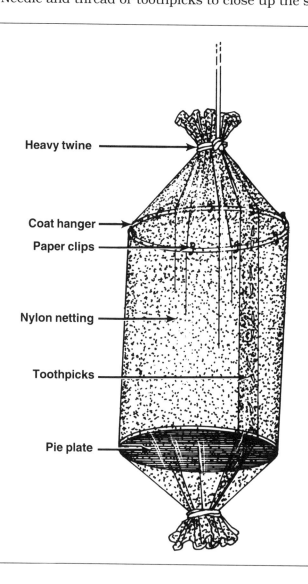

Heavy twine

Coat hanger

Paper clips

Nylon netting

Toothpicks

Pie plate

APPENDIX D

Raising a Second Generation of Butterflies

If you have discovered eggs in the cage, you are lucky. You have the opportunity to raise a second generation of butterflies and to experience the regenerative aspect of life cycles with your students.

Butterflies usually lay their eggs on the leaves of food plants favored by the larvae (caterpillars) so that the hatchlings have an instant supply of food. But they will lay them on other things too, such as paper towels. Look for the eggs, then collect them by removing the leaves or toweling from the cage. Do not try to detach the eggs from the leaves; their natural adhesive holds them firmly in place, and removing them would probably cause damage.

When the second generation hatches, they will need food immediately. Have one of the following ready:

- the leftover commercially prepared food that came with the kit, which you stored in the refrigerator

- fresh leaves of thistle, dandelion, sage, hibiscus, hollyhock, plantain, rose of Sharon, or sunflower

As you know, the ravenous caterpillars will grow quickly, as will their appetites. Be sure to have a steady supply of food available if you undertake this project.

Bibliography

References for Teachers

Audubon Society Pocket Guides. *Familiar Butterflies.* New York: Alfred A. Knopf, Inc., 1990. *Familiar Insects and Spiders.* New York: Alfred A. Knopf, Inc., 1988.

These are simple-to-use field guides that come in a convenient pocket size and have colorful illustrations.

Fischer-Nagel, Heiderose. *Life of the Butterfly.* Minneapolis: Carolrhoda Books, Inc., 1987.

Excellent full-color pictures of the stages of the butterfly life cycle. Many different species are shown.

Mitchell, Robert T., and Herbert S. Zim. *Butterflies and Moths: A Guide to the More Common American Species.* New York: Golden Press, 1977.

Another field guide that lists numerous species of butterflies and moths.

Porter, Keith. *Discovering Butterflies and Moths.* New York: The Bookwright Press, 1986.

This book provides a wealth of photographs from Oxford Scientific Films. The photographs of the life cycle, camouflage, and daily life are especially good.

Reidel, Marlene. *From Egg to Butterfly.* Minneapolis: Carolrhoda Books, Inc., 1981.

Describes metamorphosis from egg to caterpillar to pupa to adult. Clear, attractive illustrations.

Whalley, Paul. *Butterfly and Moth.* New York: Alfred A. Knopf, 1988.

Fabulous photographs and informative text.

References for Students

Cox, Rosamund Kidman, and Barbara Cork. *Usborne First Nature Butterflies and Moths.* Tulsa: EDC Publishing, 1980.

> Detailed, informative illustrations fill every page. The book includes sections on how to identify an insect, how insects keep warm, how they spend their day, mating, laying eggs, and metamorphosis.

Cutts, David. *Look, a Butterfly.* Mahwah, New Jersey: Troll Associates, 1982.

> Simple text and bright illustrations show the life cycle of a butterfly. Large pictures of monarch, buckeye, cabbage, and swallowtail butterflies.

Gibbons, Gail. *Monarch Butterfly.* New York: Holiday House, 1989.

> The story of the complete life cycle of the monarch, including its annual migration. Clear text and outstanding illustrations.

Heller, Ruth. *How to Hide a Butterfly and Other Insects.* New York: Grosset and Dunlap, 1985.

> Minimal rhyming text. Attention is focused on the illustrations, which hide cleverly camouflaged caterpillars, butterflies, moths, a praying mantis, grasshoppers, bees, and spiders.

Watts, Barrie. *Butterfly and Caterpillar.* Morristown, New Jersey: Silver Burdett Press, 1985.

> Color photographs show the complete life cycle of the cabbage white butterfly. Text includes simple bold headings and more detailed reading for the more advanced.

Children's Literature

Fisher, Aileen. *When It Comes to Bugs.* New York: Harper and Row, 1986.

> Sixteen original poems about insects and how they envision the world.

Howe, James. *I Wish I Were a Butterfly.* Orlando, Florida: Gulliver Books, Harcourt Brace Jovanovich, 1987.

> A wise spider counsels a cricket struggling with an identity problem. A lovely story to read aloud to the class.

Kent, Jack. *The Caterpillar and the Polliwog.* Englewood Cliffs, New Jersey: Prentice-Hall, 1982.

> Impressed by the caterpillar's boast that she will turn into a butterfly, a polliwog is determined to watch the caterpillar very carefully and turn into a butterfly, too.

Rosetti, Christina. *The Caterpillar*. New York: Contemporary Books, Inc., 1988.

> A pleasantly illustrated booklet of the poem, printed on thick paperboard.

Ryder, Joanne. *Where Butterflies Grow*. New York: E.P. Dutton, 1989.

> An imaginative tale of metamorphosis and how it must feel to experience it. Excellent illustrations. Provides hints about how to attract butterflies to your garden.

Viorst, Judith. *The Tenth Good Thing about Barney*. New York: Atheneum, 1971.

> A sensitive story about Barney and how everyone acted and felt when he died. Portrays death as a natural part of life.

General Reference: Other Life Cycles

Coldrey, Jennifer. *The Silkworm Story*. London: Andre Deutsch Ltd., 1983.

> Easy text and large, full-color photographs of the life of the exotic silkworm.

Coldrey, Jennifer, and Karen Goldie-Morrison (Editors). *Hide and Seek*. New York: G.P. Putnam's Sons, 1986.

> Using full-color photographs from the Oxford Scientific Film Library, the book captures nature's masters of disguise—cheetah, polar bear, iguana, moths, caterpillars, flounder, and frog—to name a few.

Hall, Donald. *Ox-Cart Man*. New York: Viking Press, 1979.

> A journey through all the seasons of the year with a nineteenth-century New England farm family.

Heller, Ruth. *Chickens Aren't the Only Ones*. New York: Grosset and Dunlap, 1981.

> A beautifully illustrated look at other egg-layers: reptiles, dinosaurs, amphibians, fish, and insects.

Nash, Pamela. *See How It Grows Series*. Cleveland: Modern Curriculum Press, 1983.

> A series of 12 booklets written in simple language and illustrating the life cycles of familiar plants and animals, such as the frog, the butterfly, the bird, the pony, the tomato, and the orange.

Selberg, Ingrid. *Nature's Hidden World.* New York: Philomel Books, 1984.

> This beautifully illustrated pop-up book features the activities and life cycles of sparrows, frogs, spiders, butterflies, bees, and moles.

Seymour, Peter. *Insects: A Close-up Look.* New York: Macmillan Publishing Co., 1984.

> An engaging pop-up book featuring the grasshopper, the mosquito, the dragonfly, and the butterfly.

Waddell, Martin. *Once There Were Giants* . New York: Delacorte Press, Bantam, Doubleday, Dell Publishing Group, Inc., 1989.

> Follows a girl from infancy to adulthood. Charming illustrations and sensitive text.

Watts, Barrie. *Dragonfly.* Englewood Cliffs, New Jersey: Silver Burdett, 1988.

> Photographs, drawings, and text on two levels show the complete life cycle of the dragonfly.

Williams, John. *The Life Cycle of a Swallow.* New York: The Bookwright Press, 1989.

> Describes the physical characteristics, habits, and life cycle of that graceful bird, the swallow.

Black Line Masters

On the following pages you will find full-page illustrations of the life cycle of the Painted Lady butterfly. The illustrations make an effective bulletin board display, or they can be reproduced for use as overhead transparencies.

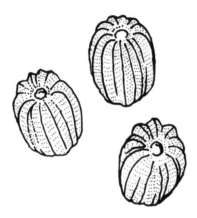

Eggs

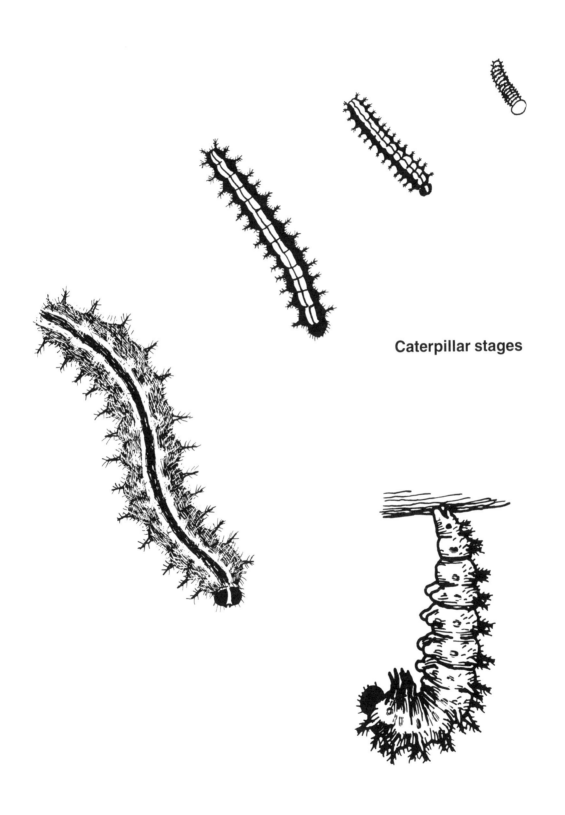

Caterpillar stages

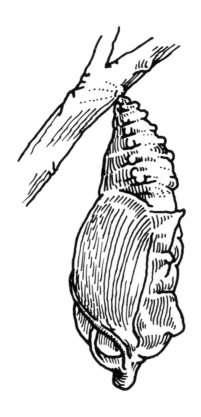

Chrysalis

Adult Painted Lady Butterfly

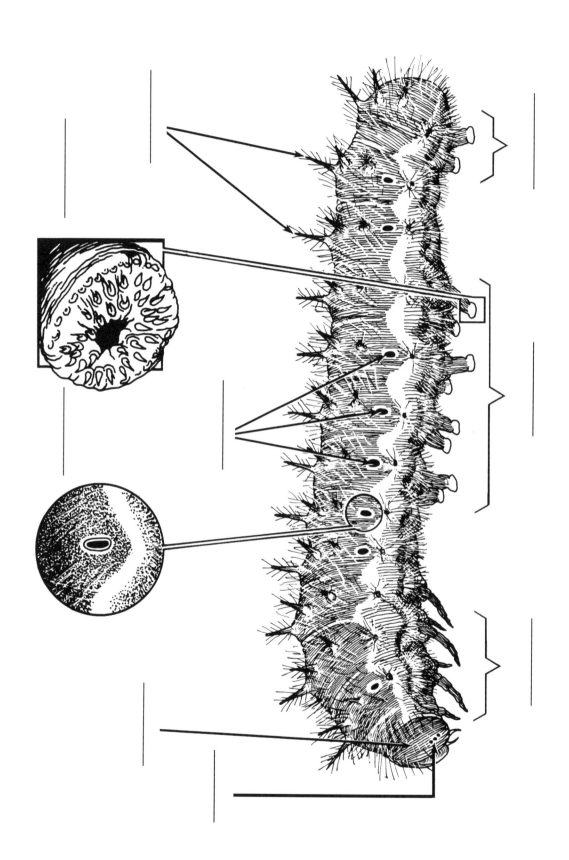

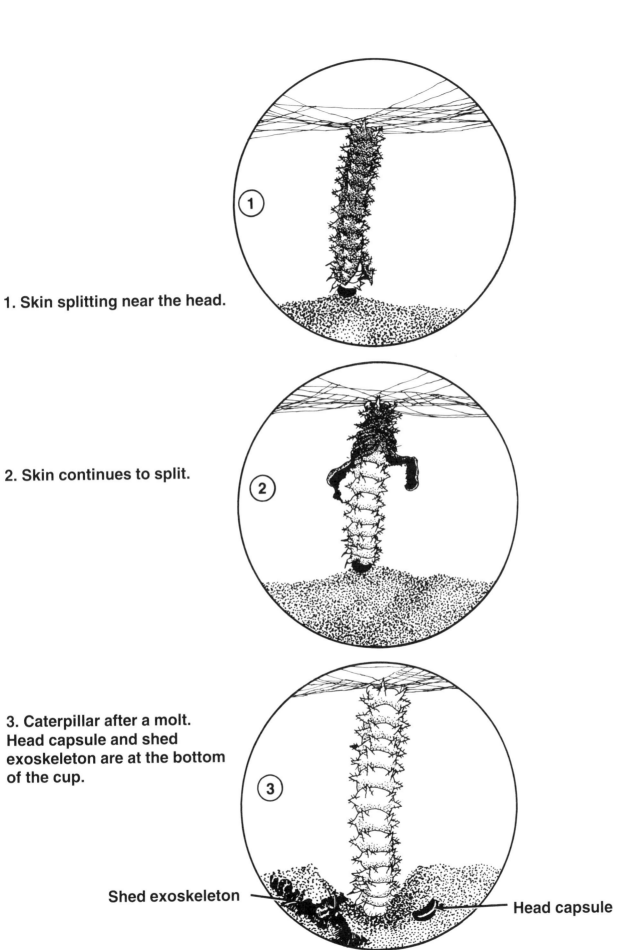

1. Skin splitting near the head.

2. Skin continues to split.

3. Caterpillar after a molt. Head capsule and shed exoskeleton are at the bottom of the cup.

Shed exoskeleton

Head capsule

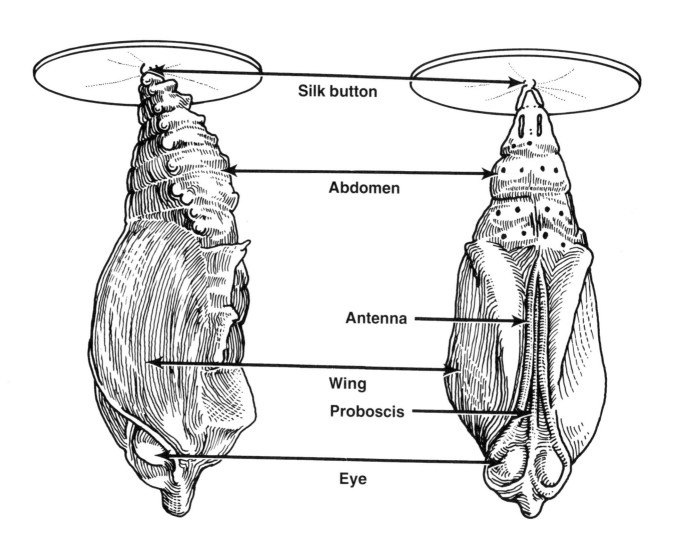

Silk button

Abdomen

Antenna

Wing

Proboscis

Eye

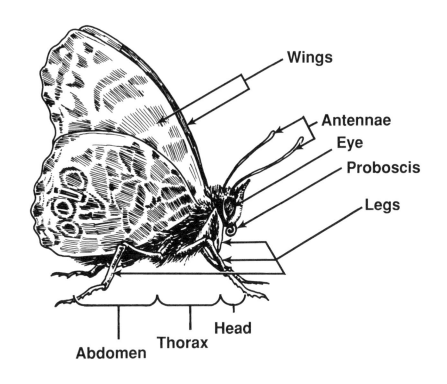

Wings

Antennae

Eye

Proboscis

Legs

Head

Thorax

Abdomen

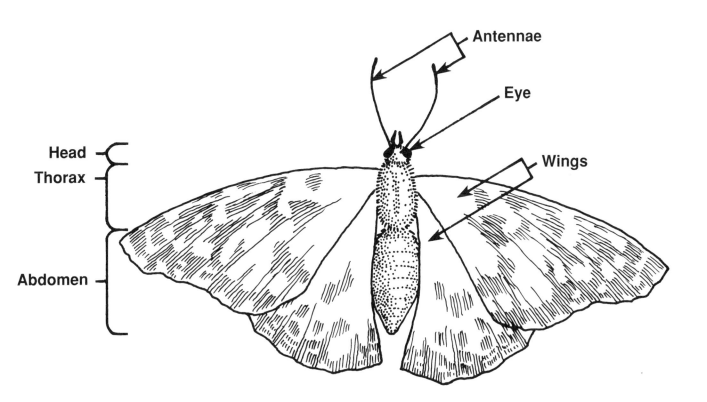

Antennae

Eye

Wings

Head

Thorax

Abdomen

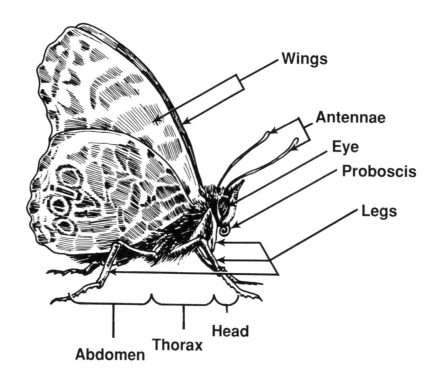

Wings

Antennae

Eye

Proboscis

Legs

Abdomen

Thorax

Head

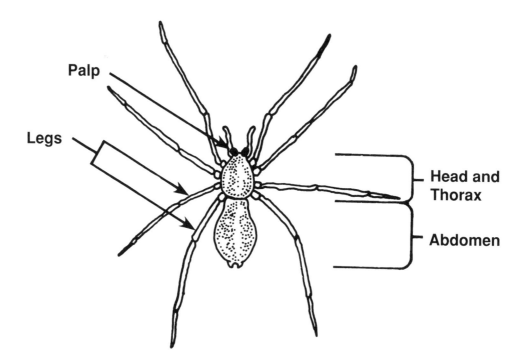

Palp

Legs

Head and Thorax

Abdomen

Materials Reorder Information

During the course of hands-on science activities, some of the materials are used up. The consumable materials from each Science and Technology for Children™ unit can be reordered as a unit refurbishment set. In addition, a unit's components can be ordered separately.

For information on refurbishing *The Life Cycle of Butterflies* or purchasing additional components, please call Carolina Biological Supply Company at **800-334-5551.**